A Walk in a Widow's Shoes

Kim Castellano

In Memory of
Jim

DEDICATION

I dedicate this book to my two beautiful daughters, Alexandra Rose Marguerite Curnyn and Samantha Lee Cecilia Curnyn. They are the loves and lights of my life and I cannot imagine living without them. They pushed me to be the best single parent that I could possibly be for which I am eternally grateful. I am so proud of the incredible, smart, funny, balanced young ladies they have become despite this tragedy.

To Jim's mom, Marianne Nappo, and his sister and brother, Lynda and Brian for welcoming and keeping me in their family.

To my furry white son, Louie, the sweetest West Highland Terrier, who gives me unconditional love and sloppy wet kisses when I need them the most.

SUMMARY

This is a guidebook for navigating the trials and tribulations of losing a loved one with all the accompanying grief. It is also my memoir. My story, my life is in these pages. I kept the chapters short for a reason– so if you can't concentrate or have no time to read, which, in the beginning, you probably won't, they can be read quickly to get the help needed as soon as possible.

In the first twenty-four hours, you need to notify family, move money out of your joint account, and breathe deeply. In the next thirty-six hours you need to find the Will, make wake/funeral arrangements and make a master list of things you will need to do over the next several days/weeks.

Know that grief only lasts for a few years; it's temporary. I know you probably don't think that now but you WILL survive your loss, slowly. You will never forget the person you lost; you will just tuck them away safely in a corner of your mind and heart forever.

I hope you find my story and the rest of this book helpful, as it was the reason I wrote it. I am not a professional grief counselor; I'm just a regular woman who had a regular life until her husband took his.

Here, in no particular order, are things that helped me:
- Loving and spending time with your children (if you have them)
- Hugs

- Friends

- Bereavement Group

- Family

- Faith

- Exercise

- Staying busy

- Yoga

- Al-Anon

- Being kind to yourself and taking time out for you

- Mourning as hard and for as long as you need to but knowing it's temporary

- Volunteer work

- Listening to music

- Nature, especially being by the ocean (water is very calming, healing)

- Pets

- Keep moving forward

- Live one hour, one minute, one second at a time, whatever works best for you to get you through your day

- Don't beat yourself up, there are no rules

In other words, try and do the very best you can every day. After a while it will come naturally and willingly with all that you have learned during this difficult time. It will be your new norm. You will smile, laugh and possibly even love again. I wish you the best of luck!

TABLE OF CONTENTS

PREFACE

Your perfect little world could change in a New York minute. Mine changed on a sunny, spring day, March 30, 2006. My morning started out like most of the rest. I got up, made our bed, then went downstairs to prepare my daughter's breakfast, packed lunch for my just-turned-seven-year-old, and walked her to the bottom of the driveway to board the bus to first grade. I came back in, cleaned up the breakfast dishes, and attempted to gather up my four-and-a-half-year-old to go grocery shopping, as it was Thursday, our grocery day. She was in the basement with my husband, Jim.

I called, "Samantha, come upstairs; you're not supposed to be down there when Daddy is working". My husband replied, "Oh, leave her, it's okay; I can't say no to that cute little face."

So I left her down there until I got dressed.

When I was ready to leave, I called down to Jim, "Hon, I'm going grocery shopping; do you need anything?"

He replied, "Razors blades and shaving cream."

I said, "Okay. I love you; see you in about an hour." He said, "I love you too."

Little did I know when I walked out the door that day, those would be his last words.

FINDING JIM

Thursday, March 30, was a lovely spring day, yet I had an unsettled feeling. I knew something was wrong; I just didn't know what.

I came home from grocery shopping and Jim did not come up from the basement to help me unload the car. Strange. I brought in the groceries and put them away. After I finished, I made my daughter her lunch.

I decided to ask Jim if he wanted me to fix him something to eat. I felt myself getting anxious. Why was my heart racing? I went downstairs to our basement, his office when he's home, and Jim was not there. The lights were on, as well as the television, and the computer.

I immediately noticed his wallet and car keys sitting on the pool table. That was odd. If his wallet and keys were there, then where was he? He couldn't be far. I went back upstairs and walked through the house. Was he in the shower? No. I checked the garage. Since it was a beautiful day, I thought, perhaps he decided to take a drive. His beloved classic car, a 1969 Oldsmobile 442 Cutlass convertible he'd named Ginger because of her gold color, was right there in her spot. Where was he? I had a nagging feeling that something was terribly wrong.

I went back downstairs to the basement and rounded the bend when I noticed out of the corner of my eye that his shop door was closed.

That was not a good sign. Why was the door closed? That door was always left partially ajar. I turned the handle; the door was locked. Why was it locked? That door was never locked. Now I was frantic. I yelled, "Jim, open the door; you're scaring me." No response.

My heart was pounding in my chest; was he in there? I stood there motionless thinking of the possibilities. My first thought was he may have passed out because he had confessed the week before that he had been drinking quite a bit lately, obviously without my knowledge. Maybe he'd hurt himself with one of his many power tools. Was he in there?

At this point, I was starting to panic and my blood literally ran cold through my veins. I was holding my breath and then I tried to breathe. I couldn't breathe!

I kicked at the door. Nothing. I kicked it again, only harder and it flew open. That's when I saw my husband Jim, slumped on the floor, his blood running down his face. I also saw a shotgun sitting by his side. There was a huge chunk of brain matter on the floor. There were also bits of brain and blood on his workshop cabinets. It's by the grace of God that somehow I didn't notice that half of the top of his head was missing.

I screamed a blood-curdling scream but I didn't go to him. By then, I knew there was nothing I could do because I was certain he was dead.

Without a pause, I ran up the stairs at top speed taking them two at a time and snatched up the phone in the kitchen. With the phone in my hand, I ran outside to our front porch, the beautiful one he built me and had just completed six months prior for our ten-year wedding anniversary. I went outside because Samantha was in the house and I didn't want her to hear me.

With trembling hands, I dialed 911 and shrieked into the phone, "My husband blew his brains out!" I kept repeating that horrific line over and over to the 911 dispatcher, and finally gave our address to her after her repeated attempts to get the information and then I hung up. Next, I dialed my neighbor and best friend, Juliette. She picked up and I screamed into the phone, "Jim blew his head off!" I kept screaming it over and over until I just hung up.

All of a sudden, I remembered that my four-and-a-half-year-old daughter was in the house. Oh my God, where was she? Just as I was about to go inside to look for her, she walked up to the entry way and locked the storm door. Perhaps she heard me scream, got frightened and decided to lock the door. I tried for several minutes to convince her to open the door and let Mama in, but she wouldn't. She just stood there and shook her head no. Oh dear Lord, would she go looking for her Daddy and see what I saw? With all my strength, I broke through the door with my shoulder and brought her outside.

Within moments, screaming sirens and flashing lights sped up my driveway. Police, EMS, and everyone was talking to me but I couldn't make sense of what they were saying. It was as if I was underwater, drowning. My friends, Juliette and Terry, who had been out for their daily walk together, came tearing across my lawn to me. Terry took my daughter next door to Juliette's.

Juliette sat with me on my cold, hard slate walkway in front of my house.

The police started asking me routine questions. Did we fight? Had we been arguing? What was his state of mind prior to that day? Oh dear God, did they think I killed him? Juliette put a pill in my mouth and told me to swallow. I remained seated on the ground in shock.

On that day, March 30, 2006 at approximately 12:45 p.m., my life as I knew it changed forever.

PINE BOX

To me, the worst part of the death of someone dear to you, other than the fact you will never see that loved one again, is to see them put in a box, then buried deep in the ground. I never liked basements, subways or tunnels. Even as a kid, the mere thought of going underground for all eternity, to me, was petrifying.

That being said, I made my burial intentions known to my husband early on in our marriage. I clearly, and on more than one occasion, stated that I did not want to be placed in the ground.

I would say, "I would like a one-day wake, a Catholic Church funeral service, with a full mass and beautiful hymns." I even knew the hymns I wanted to be played.

"Shortly thereafter, I said, "I want to be cremated. Or, skip the wake entirely, have me cremated, have a beautiful mass and then a celebration of my life. If we skip straight to the cremation," I continued to ramble, "I certainly won't need a fancy coffin because it wasn't going to be needed longer than the service. What you do with me after I am cremated would depend. If we have children, and they want to keep my ashes in an urn, that will be fine."

However, if not, I would like my ashes to be sprinkled in the Gulf of Mexico in front of our family condo. Either way, no burial. Simple, straight to the point. Case closed."

Jim thought I was crazy. He would say I was being morbid but I would say I was just being prepared. Plus, I wanted to make damn sure I wasn't going in the ground.

When I would ask my husband how and where he would like to be buried, he would always say, "Bury me in a pine box close to home."

Are you serious? I'd say. He would reply, "Yes." That's what he said time and time again.

Jim was very easy going and liked things pretty simple and basic. So, when he died and it came time for me to go to the funeral home and pick out his casket, I was thinking about what I would actually do.

I asked myself, "Should I honor his wish? How can I buy him a pine box? Won't that look tacky? What will people think? Then I came to my senses and said, "Why should I care what people think."

Okay, maybe not a pine box but I would find something simple, yet tasteful. If only we were Jewish, I mused, he could have his pine box and no one would question his decision.

Because Jim died so young and so suddenly, I had no time to prepare. I was paralyzed with grief especially when my brother came to my house to take me to the funeral home; I found myself immobile. I have vague memories of that day, and recall being ushered into a room that smelled very medicinal. A rather cold, business-like funeral director sat me down in an uncomfortable chair across from a large wooden desk. I sat on the right, my brother on my left.

The funeral director was dressed in a dark-colored suit, starch-white shirt and mundane tie. He was dressed appropriately for his line of work. Next, he cleared his throat then expressed his condolences. I must say that he tried to sound sincere but I knew it was his job to appear sympathetic and compassionate. I knew instantly that he was anything but those things. I was merely a client, a customer and he was about to make a sale. And it became a rather large sale.

So, here we were sitting in this office about to go over the arrangements and expenses regarding Jim's wake and funeral.

Let me tell you up front that if you don't have at least $10,000 set aside for your loved one's full-fledged funeral, you should start saving now. Besides the ridiculous cost of caskets, there are so many other fees involved. There are the usual expenses for flowers, limo, the church, the organist, and the burial plot. But, how many of us think about items such as embalming fees?

You will also have to pay to feed your guests after the service. And don't forget: once the ground settles, you will have to decide on and purchase a headstone.

The headstone alone can and has caused great rifts within a family. Other widows and widowers I know each have their own story. I know my mother-in-law wasn't happy that I didn't include her in the choice of headstone or consulted with her on the wording. She never said anything to me. But when she purchased a bench on the boardwalk near her home in Long Beach, New York, she basically excluded me and my daughters, causing one daughter to say when she read it, "We've been reduced to 'family'".

On my late husband's headstone, I placed his full name, the day, date and year he was born and the same for his death. Under that, I wrote Beloved Husband and Father. The next line says Dedicated Lion as Jim was the youngest Lion in my town's history and he took incredible pride in being called a Lion. My older daughter, Alexandra, wanted a cross added and Samantha requested a heart. At the very bottom, I had "Shine On" from the song, "Shine On You Crazy Diamond" by his favorite band, Pink Floyd.

Are you being cremated? If you are, like me, you can have your family buy a used casket. Perhaps the casket has been previously used to host a wake before a cremation. Why not purchase one? It's a fraction of the cost and you're not going to be needing it. It seems to be the most practical way of doing things, if you ask me.

My husband was an organ donor—so it read on his Driver's License. It was never mentioned, however, and I certainly didn't think of it. If his wishes had been followed, I would not have had to worry about a casket, plot or even a headstone. We could have saved close to $15,000. Not one cent would he live to enjoy.

But back to the funeral director. Before "Mr. Morose" launched into his spiel he said, "Jim's body is here now," which caused me to burst into tears. Hearing those words made this nightmare a grim reality. Next, he callously slid something to me across the desk. It took me a moment to process what it was and then I absolutely lost it. It was Jim's wedding band; the only jewelry my husband wore after we got married. That cruel act was obviously necessary, as he had to return my husband's ring; however, the manner in which he did it was so incredibly callous. The whole return of "property" could have been handled more delicately.

Once I collected myself and we went over the floral arrangements, the limousine and the other details, it was time to go look at caskets. My mother-in-law and brother-in-law had been waiting in the waiting area and now joined my brother and me as we exited the office.

I know I should have gone with them to look at the multitude of caskets in another room, but I was still reeling from my husband's sudden death and I couldn't deal with coffins. I don't know if it was because I am terrified of caskets, which symbolize going in the ground, or because it would make his death real.

Either way, I didn't budge. My brother, mother-in-law and brother-in-law went to look at the selections and decide.

After about a half hour or so, or so I thought—frankly, it could have been ten minutes or two hours as I suddenly had no concept of time—they came back in the room. My mother-in-law had picked out a hand-carved mahogany casket with beautiful brass detail.

Mahogany. The most expensive wood you can buy.

Jim loved to work with wood. He built our back deck, our front porch, our mantelpiece, our bar, bookshelves, you name it. I guess she thought mahogany would be a good choice because it was a beautiful wood, one that he would like.

Please recall, Jim wanted to be buried in a pine box but now he would be buried in a mahogany casket, to be paid for by me, the widow. Somehow that didn't seem right, or fair, but I nodded in agreement only because if I hadn't, I would have had to go in the casket room and chose his eternal resting vessel myself. That was something I knew I couldn't possibly do.

I got spared that decision, but at what price?

Eight thousand dollars to be exact.

THE JACKIE O WIDOW

Grief and the grieving process is the most painful experience that any spouse, parent or child can endure.

There are many ways to grieve. Some people sob uncontrollably. Being Italian, I can tell you from my experience that Italians are very emotional and grieve loudly. We don't just sob; we wail and scream and sometimes even faint. I have seen grandmothers and aunts of mine do all of the above. I have even seen one or two throw themselves on the body or coffin while screaming, "Why wasn't it me?"

Then, there are others who simply weep quietly. They are basically so numb that they barely register emotion.

Then there is what I call the Jackie O Widow. A Jackie O Widow is a woman who shows little or no emotion. They attend the wakes, greet mourners and smile and nod pleasantly when spoken to. Their mascara is perfectly intact at the end of the day. They maintain a flawless face.

Don't get me wrong, I'm sure they grieve, but just not publicly. Is it because they are numb or are they simply being stoic?

My mom was a Jackie O Widow. She would never show public displays of emotion. I, on the other hand, for the first time in my life, wasn't anything like her. At my husband's wake and funeral, I cried and cried often. My face was etched with grief. My nose and mascara both ran and I used a ridiculous amount of tissues.

Since Jim's death was so sudden, I was still in total shock days later. When it came time for the wake and funeral, I only remember bits and pieces. I do remember not being the first one at the wake because I basically didn't want to go. I took my time getting dressed. My family kept yelling upstairs to me saying we needed to leave, or we would be late which is exactly what ended up happening. Out of respect for me, the first set of mourners waited outside.

Speaking of dressing, make sure you wear something you're not fond of because you will never wear it again. Jim's mother actually burned her outfit after the funeral.

For obvious reasons, Jim had a closed coffin. Even if my husband hadn't blown his brains out, as I had bluntly come to say, I still would have had a closed coffin, which is very rare for an Italian. I just never thought the person looked the same in death as they had in life, so I would much rather remember that person the way they were, rather than as a painted, stiff version of themselves.

I remember being in the second set of chairs because my mother-in-law took my seat: the first seat is always reserved for the widow.

My family took turns sitting beside me. Mostly my sister Laura sat with me and so did her oldest son Paul. My closest friends sat in rows directly behind me. I remember waves of people coming to greet me. Some of the mourners I remember vividly. One in particular comes to mind. He was a friend of my husband's, named Rick, who he met through The Lions Club.

He is a tall man, well over six feet tall and he literally fell to his knees and sobbed like a baby in my lap. Others I didn't even remember being there until I looked at the sign-in book many months later.

Another thing that I didn't remember was what my dear friend Amy, who watched my girls when I went to the night wake, told me. Apparently, I would say, "I know" to everyone who came up to me to extend their condolences; a phrase I still say ten long years later.

Thankfully, I had a one-day wake. The usual hours, 2:00 – 4:00 p.m., 7:00 – 9:00 p.m. Some people thrust themselves into the agony of a two-day wake. Fortunately, I had enough common sense to know that two days of repeating "I know" and "thank you" would be too much. The two sessions were brutal. I felt physically and emotionally exhausted after the first round and have no idea to this day how I made it through the second one.

The funeral was on a chilly, gray day. My girls, being seven and four were thrilled to ride in the big, shiny, black limousine. We pulled up to our little, sweet, one-hundred-year-old church and I immediately had to go to the ladies' room.

Without meaning to, I held everyone up. When we were ready to enter, I held my girls' hands as we slowly followed the coffin up the center aisle. All eyes were on us. Then, of course, we sat in the first row. My brother Peter and Jim's sister Lynda read from the bible and the organist played all the hymns I requested.

Mid-service, my husband's cousin Anthony got up and spoke about Jim. He told stories of all the silly things he used to do, especially with our girls. When he mentioned how Jim loved to roll them up in blankets and pretend that they were tortillas, my oldest, Alexandra, absolutely lost it and sobbed uncontrollably in my lap for the rest of the service.

Walking back down the aisle, trailing the coffin after the service, felt like an eternity. Everyone just gazed in our direction. They all looked at us with wide-eyed, blank stares. Again, I made everyone wait as I needed to make another trip to the ladies' room. The kidneys react to fear, and I was fearful of what lay ahead.

We piled back into the limo and made the five-minute trip to the cemetery. I wish I'd had enough forethought to ask the driver to go past the house first before proceeding to the cemetery. One of the few things I would have done differently.

We pulled in and walked a few feet to the grave site. I had no idea where Jim was being interred until that exact moment, as I did not pick out the plot, my dear friend and neighbor, Juliette did.

How could I let someone pick the place my husband would spend eternity? Well, first, I was in such a state of shock that, frankly, I couldn't wrap my head around any details. Juliette and her husband, Paul, Jim's best friend, even picked out the suit my husband would wear in his coffin. Second, with two small children, it was almost impossible to find the time to go looking at plots. Third, and most importantly, I have and have always had a fear of death, particularly of going in the ground. So, to me, looking at a burial plot for my late husband was not even an option.

I had wanted him buried in a Catholic cemetery but, since that side of the cemetery was full, he had to be buried in a non-denominational plot. I knew he wouldn't care, as long as he got his wish and was buried in our town, close to home.

My two favorite priests, Father George and Monsignor Moore, were so kind and I'm sure they said lovely things but I have no idea to this day what they said. When the service ended, my girls let go of their daddy balloons. What is a daddy balloon? When my girls were little, and we had just returned home from a carnival, one of their balloons escaped their grasp and flew away. Of course, they started to cry. All of a sudden, a thought popped into my head. I said, "Don't cry, the balloon went to Heaven to see Poppy." Poppy was my father, whom they knew all about but had never met. From that moment on, whenever they got a balloon, they would set it free for Poppy. So, when Jim died, we decided that they would release balloons at the funeral for Daddy. This time, we took it one step further. With a Sharpie pen, I had them write a message to Daddy on each of their balloons.

Samantha, being four-and-a-half, just scribbled a heart on hers. Alexandra, who had been reading since age three, wrote the most heartbreaking message on hers. A message that reduced everyone who read it to tears. To this day, I wish I could remember what she wrote. Their simple act of letting their balloons go made everyone cry. It was a heartbreaking but touching moment.

I highly recommend Daddy, Mommy, Grandma, Grandpa, or whomever balloons for children to release. From that day on, we would continue to write on them and send them up for birthdays, anniversaries, Father's Day, or any other holiday. I told many of my friends who are widowed with children about this and several, if not all, adopted my idea.

After the funeral service, the funeral director made an announcement that a reception was to follow at our home. I wish I hadn't been catatonic and had personally asked everyone to come, even the priests, as not too many people came and there was enough food for an army, thanks again to my incredible neighbors, Paul and Juliette.

When the guests piled into our home and started making plates of food or pouring themselves drinks, I remember going upstairs. I took off my heels and put on my slippers. I sat outside neither eating nor drinking despite the many food pushers who surrounded me. I sat wrapped in a blanket talking to my friends and family who smoked. They were the only ones brave enough to sit outside on that damp, raw April day.

I was thoroughly numb at this point, no longer crying as I had no more tears left to cry.

Or, had I turned into a Jackie O widow?

WATCH OUT FOR THE MEAL TRAIN

If you don't know what I refer to as "the meal train," you will, once your spouse or family member dies. The meal train is a never-ending parade of trays wrapped in tin foil carried by people who stop by your home, with food in hand, and sometimes with no warning.

People want to do something for you, anything, to help you even if it's only in a small way. Friends and family feel helpless and by reaching out, I believe it is their way of giving comfort especially with food. This must be where the term "comfort food" was derived.

Who are these people? Family, friends, and neighbors usually are the first to start the meal train; however, acquaintances and even complete strangers may also participate, depending on whether your community is tight-knit. My daughter Samantha's preschool and my oldest daughter Alexandra's Girl Scout troop both started meal trains. While I knew and was even friendly with some of the other moms and stay-at-home dads, there were quite a few I didn't know. That fact didn't stop them from coming by my home and dropping off food.

Some of the food was homemade and lovingly prepared, while some was catered from local restaurants. The thing that amazed me was it wasn't just a dish, like a casserole. Sometimes it was a full blown meal with bread, salad and even dessert. I will never forget my friend Nancy's husband, Brian, walking up my driveway. I was standing outside for whatever reason, and found it sweet, yet odd when he handed me a tray of chicken Parmesan. He looked at me with tears in his eyes, gave me a brief hug, mumbled his sympathies then literally hung his head and slowly descended my driveway.

The week after Jim died, I had to put a stop to the meal train for various reasons. The first one being that I am Italian and with Italians, especially my family, it's always been and always will be all about the food. Food, at least to me, is like drinking. It comes with celebration so, during my mourning period, I had a very hard time eating anything at all. I ate because I had to, or at least everyone kept telling me I had to, especially since I lost twelve pounds, going down to a mere 114 pounds after the wake and funeral.

At 5'5" that was not a healthy weight for me. I looked terrible; my face looked sallow and my cheeks were hollow. I needed a belt to keep my pants up. It was sad that I ate out of necessity, not because I wanted to, nor was I enjoying it. Now, my friends and even strangers wanted me to accept their food, which was basically impossible for me.

Second, who is going to eat all that food? There was, and usually is, enough food dropped off to feed an army (my favorite saying). I know, firsthand, that some of it gets eaten the first few days as your family, in-laws and out of town relatives and friends are around for the wake and funeral and meals end up being at your home. After that, you end up with a refrigerator full of rotting food. You can only freeze some of it, which I did, but a freezer, or even two in my case, will only hold so much. Then what? A friend of mine who lost his wife, actually rented a small freezer so he could freeze the abundant amount of meals given to him. He was thrilled that he didn't have to cook for weeks. It was one less thing for him to think about. A great idea actually, especially if you are a man or a woman who hates to cook.

I don't know about you, but one of my biggest pet peeves is wasting food. I was raised that way and, in addition, was a poor eater as a child which is amazing to me as I truly love food now. Yes, I'm a foodie, and would much rather go to a five-star restaurant than buy a designer bag or a beautiful pair of shoes.

Since I was such a terrible eater and just basically pushed my food around my plate, I spent many nights in my family kitchen watching my mother clean our kitchen while my dinner got cold and actually congealed on my plate. Obviously, I had no choice but to nip the meal train in the bud quickly before I had to start tossing out great quantities of food, which would have depressed me further.

I must say, the meal train is a nice gesture, but should only provide meals three or four times per week rather than every day. If you like to cook, like I do, the meal train can do more harm than good. I find cooking soothing, and I like to chop vegetables, as I think it is therapeutic. Taking that away from me, albeit with all good intentions, made my grieving harder, as I lost an outlet. It allowed me to think more as I had more time on my hands. You definitely don't want to think more as you are already doing enough of that!

In addition, I am a bit of a germaphobe, especially when it comes to food. I have had food poisoning twice and I can tell you that it's a horrific experience and I certainly will spare you the details. I must admit I was very leery about eating home cooking, especially when it was from someone I didn't know well. Are they clean people? Do they have cats walking on the kitchen counter while they are preparing food? I shudder to think. Okay, say it, I'm a food snob.

Guilty as charged.

Truth be told, my children, like I was, are picky eaters so it's very difficult to cook for someone you don't know extremely well. If you give them a gift card to a local restaurant or pizzeria, they can at least order food that they will eat. I have to say, the best thing we received, at least in my girls' eyes, was when a cookie basket was delivered brimming with dozens of cookies, mostly chocolate chip, my girls' favorite.

If you want to give a gift to a bereaved family, especially one with young children, I highly recommend it as it was the first smile I had seen on their little faces in many days.

What if your spouse was a woman? I was told by several male friends of mine who'd lost their wives that they not only appreciated the food but welcomed it. Feeding their family became one less thing to tackle, especially since they weren't domestic types.

Since Jim's death ten years ago, meal trains have gotten sophisticated; they are frequently offered online. A person can set up a meal train for anyone, not just for a bereaved family. Now they are set up for new parents, people with illnesses and surgery patients just to name a few. How do I know about this? My friend Michelle, who is a nurse practitioner, has two friends, a husband and wife, who are both battling cancer. While she desperately wanted to provide them with a home cooked meal or two, she couldn't because of her busy work schedule. So she asked me to sign up online and prepare two meals for them.

Now you can go to a person's secure page, find out their likes and dislikes, their food allergies and then you can put yourself on a schedule to cook a meal. You will be asked to type in what meal you are cooking so they don't get duplicates. Amazing. So, whether you like it or not, you will probably experience the meal train. You can give food away to some friends and then freeze as much as you can for another day. The rest is a decision you will have to make at some point. What you do with the rest of the food and how you handle it are entirely up to you.

What is it about food that makes people come together, whether in celebration or sorrow? As my friend Juliette and I always say, "It's all about the food."

STUPID THINGS PEOPLE SAY

When your loved one dies, people say the most inappropriate things. I don't know why, but they do. Perhaps people feel like they have to say something—anything that sounds like words of wisdom. Frankly, I think it's because death makes people extremely uncomfortable and they feel the need to fill the silence. Why can't people just say something as simple as, "I'm sorry for your loss." My friends and I were truly amazed.

Here are a few choice sayings people imparted to me shortly after my late husband's death. The first stupid thing people say is at the wake when there is an open casket. Thankfully, Jim's was closed, as were my parents'. I was fortunate that I didn't have to hear anyone say, "*He/She looks good.*" Really? How good could they possibly look; they are dead!

"*All things happen for a reason.*" This saying is the worst of all time but especially after someone dies. All things happen for a reason? And what might that reason be? My husband killed himself. Shot himself in the head. I found him. What exactly was the reason he did this? Why did he do it in our home? Was there a reason for that because, if there was, I would like to know the reason. What is the reason my life and my two daughters' lives have been forever altered?

"*Time heals all wounds.*" Oh really. How much time are we talking about? It's been ten long years since Jim's death and I can honestly say the pain has lessened but, let's be honest, I am certainly not healed or whole. Rose Kennedy summed it up best. She said, "It has been said time heals all wounds. I do not agree. The wounds remain. In time, the mind, protecting its sanity, covers them with scar tissue and the pain lessens but it is never gone." Brilliant statement and one hundred percent accurate.

"Is there anything I can do?" Yes, actually. Build me a time machine so I can go back in time and try and prevent this tragedy. What could someone possibly do? It's certainly a nice thought. Emotionally, maybe you can just visit with me and if I feel like crying, let me. If I feel like screaming, let me scream. If I simply want you to sit beside me without either of us saying a word, let me sit there in silence. If I needed some kind of help other than emotional, I am the kind of person who won't ask. If you truly want to help me, do something for me without me asking. Have my driveway plowed, rake my lawn, send your husband over if he's handy and ask if there is anything he can repair.

"You're young, you will meet someone else." What on God's green earth makes you think I want to meet someone else? I just buried my husband! What if I don't want to meet anyone else? Also, I guess being young guarantees I will meet someone else. What if I were older? That doesn't apply?

How about these beauties?

"Did he leave you insurance?

"Can you keep the house?"

"Don't worry, you can always go on welfare!"

24

These were all said to me a few days after my husband died. First of all, it is none of your business if we had insurance or whether or not I will be able to keep my house. Welfare? What a wonderful idea. What, exactly, is my alternative? Are you offering me to come live with you and your family? Doubtful.

"God only gives you what you can handle." Really? This one floors me, especially being raised Catholic. I don't understand how God thought I could handle seeing my husband's brains on the floor of our basement. Or how I could raise two little girls by myself. Or run a house, do all his chores, and look for a job too.

"Well, at least you have your girls." Yes, yes I do. My beautiful little girls who are four-and-a-half and seven who now have no father. Who were only able to say "Daddy" for those few short years and will never be able to utter the word to him again. Who will never have him teach them to ride a bike, hammer a nail or, more importantly, who will never walk them down the aisle at their weddings. Yes, I have my girls, but now I am their father as well. So unfair.

"What are you going to do with his stuff?" Why? Do you want something? People ask because they want something, especially things you will never use like his golf clubs, humidor, or suits. When my friend Keith lost his wife, her sister almost immediately after her death said she wanted her shoes! Can you imagine?

The "unclaimed" personal effects of the deceased brings out the worst in people. If you haven't experienced it yet, it's possible that you may unfortunately.

"You need to move on." Are you kidding me? Move on to what?

"When are you going to be over it?" Excuse me? Umm, never. My brother's wife had the gall to ask him that a few weeks after our beloved mother died.

Disgusting.

Be prepared to respond to very inappropriate questions. Depending upon who asked me the question and what the question was, my answers varied.

Here are some HELPFUL things that were said after Jim died:

"It's okay to get mad." Hearing this validated my feelings. I not only had a right to be sad but I also had the right to be mad. Jim left me. Even though I know he must have been clinically depressed and in a great deal of pain, he still left me. He chose to leave me and our beautiful girls. I remember yelling and screaming so loud at him, while in my car two days after I found him, that I had to pull over to the side of the road. The car is a great place to scream. If the windows are up, no one can hear you.

"He's in a better place." First of all, even though it's a cliché, I truly believe he is in a better place because of my religious background. I also desperately want to believe he's in a better place because it helps me cope. Obviously, he was in a tremendous amount of pain so anywhere but here has to be better.

"Let your children be your strength." Your children, no matter how old, are your strength. Even though mine were very young, they gave me the strength to keep going. If you weren't blessed with children, let your close friends and family be your strength so you can keep moving forward, day by day.

BETTER THINGS TO SAY & DO

As I mentioned in the last chapter, people can say and do really ignorant things when your loved one dies. They don't usually mean to say anything hurtful or silly, but death makes people uncomfortable; they don't know what to say but feel they must say something – anything, stupid or not. To me, unless you have walked a mile in those horrible bereaved shoes, the less said the better. If you feel you absolutely must say something, here are some suggestions of better things to say and/or do for your grieving friend or relative.

"It wasn't your fault." Since my late husband's death was a suicide, that was very important for me to hear, even though, rationally, I knew it wasn't my fault. He suffered from a mental illness. There is a small part of you, or in some cases, like my friend, also named Jim, a large part of you, that thinks otherwise.

I thought, "How could I have lived with this person, my spouse, and not known the depth of his pain?" I racked my brain for months trying to remember the last few weeks of my late husband's life. Was he behaving differently? Were there tell-tale signs and I just didn't see them? I thought, "Why didn't I do something?" In a chapter called, "The Effects of Alcohol," I tell you how I actually tried to do something when I recognized the problem. I offered to take him to a nearby psychiatric hospital less than ten days before he took his life, but he *wouldn't* go.

He was more worried about how he would explain this to everyone; his boss, his mother, our girls. I came up with logical excuses for all of them, but, in the end, he didn't go.

So, yes, there are days where you can't help but blame yourself. You will beat yourself up time and time again. Those few simple words, *"It wasn't your fault"* were a godsend and important for me to hear, as it took a little bit of weight off of my shoulders.

"It's okay to get mad." That simple line gave me permission to pull over to the side of the road one day and bang on my steering wheel and scream, "Why?" Why?" "Why?" "How could you do this to me?" "To us?" "To our family?" You will wonder how you can be mad at someone you loved who died, no matter how he or she died. Well, you can and you may and if you are, you have to let it out. Bottling up your emotions isn't healthy and will manifest itself in other ways (more about this in my chapter, "The Five Stages, Part II").

If your loved one died by suicide, you will be angry for years. I still get mad at him ten years later, especially when I have to take out the garbage or shovel the driveway. I am sure people have gone by my house in the winter and have seen me shaking my fist or snow shovel at the Heavens, ranting and raving at him. Being angry doesn't make you a bad person, it makes you human.

Here are some suggestions of what people could do for you:

- Give gift cards to local restaurants that deliver instead of preparing a meal. I am a pretty good cook and I am incredibly picky so, while I know people were trying to help by preparing meals (see "Watch Out for the Meal Train" chapter), unless you knew me intimately and you knew what my family and I like, a gift card is so much more practical.

- Because you get inundated with food immediately after word gets out, cook a nice meal several MONTHS after a friend's spouse has died. It's appreciated that much more once they have settled into real life and an even more hectic schedule.

- As I mentioned in the previous chapter titled, "Watch Out for the Meal Train", give a cookie basket to a family with young children. You can purchase one or make it yourself. Either way, a huge hit and greatly appreciated.

- Another great idea for families who have young children is to fill a basket with coloring books, washable markers, crayons, and other small toys. Someone made one for my girls, which kept them occupied at the funeral home, the service and reception. Again, incredibly thoughtful and wonderfully helpful. I highly recommend this.

- Believe it or not, a great thing to drop off at someone's home when you hear of their loss is what I call "the trifecta." The trifecta consists of bottled water, tissues and toilet paper. All three will come in extremely handy. Water to stay hydrated. Tissues for all the tears. Toilet paper for all the visiting guests. All three will be very appreciated and certainly won't go to waste.

I personally don't think you should tell someone who is grieving to call you if they need anything. Nine times out of ten they won't call; they will suffer in silence, especially if that person is very strong and proud. I know I never did follow up on those offers. I would never ask for help as I have been on my own since I was seventeen and I'm incredibly independent. I know I could have asked for help and would have gotten a loving response. Instead, I suggest trying to anticipate what that person might need and just do it!

If it's snowing, have someone go to their home and shovel their driveway. That type of offer also works in the fall for raking their lawn and in the summer for cutting their grass. All appreciated.

Ironically, it seemed that the minute my husband died, everything in the house started falling apart. Many of the jobs were little jobs but they needed attention. My neighbor David showed up one day with his tool belt and asked me what needed to be fixed. That was the most wonderful gift, especially since my late husband was incredibly handy, and to see everything falling apart made me even more sad and depressed.

If a male friend lost his wife, drop off some groceries and/or a few homemade pasta sauces you've made so he can throw together a quick meal after work. But most important of all, take your bereaved friend's or relative's lead. If he or she is quiet, just sit with them and do not talk. Hold their hand. To me, the best gift is to be **normal**. Talk about your life as they will want to take a break from their grief.

My friend, Nancy made me and my girls affirmation boxes. She bought three pretty boxes and wrote beautiful thoughts and sayings on little pieces of paper and put them in each box. The words inside said *you are special, someone is praying for you, smile,* etcetera. We were instructed to read one a day which we did for many months. I will never forget this. A truly great idea.

Years later, we all still have our boxes in our bedrooms. They would be very easy to create for anyone and, if you know them well, you can tailor the sayings to fit that person perfectly.

It is also good to say something that will make your friend laugh; yes, LAUGH or anything to at least make your friend/relative in mourning smile.

Believe it or not, you will feel guilty, yes, guilty the first time you laugh because you feel you shouldn't. If you are the bereaved person, you may feel you don't deserve to, nor should you smile or laugh. However, once you do it, you will take a break from your grief and it will help you feel a bit happy, even normal again, if only for a brief moment.

THE FIVE STAGES – PART I

You've heard it said before: grief has five stages. Well, having experienced them all I can tell you that it is not some psychobabble. It is pure fact. First, there is denial. Even if your loved one has been sick for many months, even years and you know the inevitable is coming, there is still denial. I know that it's a defense mechanism, as the reality is way too much to bear.

The pain is so raw that denial helps you momentarily cope. When my husband died, I used to pretend he was on a business trip. It was easy to do since he travelled a lot and had a closed casket. Obviously, I knew he was dead, but this little trick helped me keep going, even if only for a moment.

With denial and death comes an abnormal amount of stress. If you are in denial and are incredibly overwhelmed by your spouse's or loved one's death, your body may start manifesting all kinds of maladies.

Here are a few examples of what happened to me. First, I lost my voice. It was so bad that I could barely whisper to the mourners. My girlfriend, Juliette, had me drinking an awful tasting tea from China named Loquat, for days. I must admit that it helped, but it tasted terrible.

Next I developed a severe sty in my right eye. My eye was so badly infected that it was basically swollen shut. I had to visit three different eye doctors before they found the right combination of drops that finally cured it.

My next issue was a gastrointestinal condition called diverticulitis. I was scheduled for a colonoscopy four days after my husband died but because I had to deal with Jim's death and all the other issues besides the funeral, I had to postpone the procedure for a few weeks. My colon had formed a large number of pockets which were infected and inflamed. If you read anything about colons in a holistic book, you will learn that colon issues are all about letting go. Ironic.

Lastly, I was having lunch with my younger daughter at her favorite restaurant when all of a sudden, my throat started to swell on the right side. It blew up quickly and so much so that it looked like I swallowed a golf ball. My immediate thought was that I was having an allergic reaction to something I just ate. So, I had all the food, especially my daughter's beloved dumplings and rice, packed up to go and drove myself to the hospital which, thankfully, was just down the road.

I had an immediate CAT scan and it turned out that, not only did I have a stone in my salivary gland, which I still have to this day, I also developed two small kidney stones as well. All the crying had led to dehydration which caused these conditions.

So, my advice to you is to do whatever you can to cope. Find your favorite means to de-stress— whatever that is for you. I took long walks, did yoga, worked out, sank into frequent long, hot baths and regularly talked to my friends. Find things that will work for YOU.

The next stage of grief is anger. With Jim's particular type of death comes an enormous amount of anger. How could he do this to me? To our daughters? His mother? Some days, when I was particularly angry at him, I would go to the cemetery and scream at his headstone. I don't do it anymore but his mother still does it to this day.

The third stage is bargaining. The "what ifs," as I like to call them. What if I had put him in the car the night he broke down crying? Would he still be alive? About a week before Jim died I found him in his home office with headphones on, listening to music, sobbing. I asked what was wrong and he said he was a mess, that he had been drinking a lot lately and had been hiding it from me. I asked him how much was a lot and he said, "I sometimes drink in the morning or afternoon." This came as a complete and utter shock to me. I asked him if he wanted help and he replied that he did. The next morning, I had a list of no less than twenty Alcoholics Anonymous meetings within a fifteen-mile radius of our house. For people who lost their spouses or friends or relatives to cancer or an illness, I'm sure they have thought: "What if I had used a different doctor or hospital"? I am sure you get my point.

Then there is depression. I must admit, if it weren't for my girls, I would have stayed in bed for days on end, not eating or caring. I would have just slept the days away. By the way, sleeping too much is a big sign of depression—something Jim was doing a great deal of before he took his life. I thank God for my girls every day. They made me wake up, fix breakfast, grocery shop, cook our dinner. They made me be present and accountable. I didn't have a choice.

The final stage of grief is acceptance. This is a particularly hard step and I believe some people never achieve it. I had to accept Jim's death. I had to accept there was a reason he took his own life. I had to learn to forgive him so I could heal and move forward. I must admit it took me several years to get there but, thankfully, because of my faith and the help of professionals, I got there.

So, you have gone through each stage and you think you are through.

Wrong.

They start over and over again like a horrible roller coaster. Grief is cyclical. Surviving what I call "the year of firsts", first birthday without them, first anniversary, first Christmas, etc. frankly, is a tremendous feat. You think it will get easier now that you've made it through that first year. Wrong again. I hate to say this, but it actually gets worse, if that's possible. Here's how I've explained it to my family and friends.

The first year you are in complete shock; denial at best. You are living on auto pilot, doing things by rote. People will tell you things you said or did and you will have absolutely no recollection of them.

During the second year, you are very busy. In addition to your previous chores, you have now added your deceased loved one's work. In my case, paying the bills, taking out the trash and taking care of our acre of property. The hurt is ever-present but you are almost too busy, and a great deal of time, too tired to grieve. By the way, grief in itself is exhausting.

To me, the third year is the hardest. You are no longer grieving; you are in mourning. Reality sets in. This is your new life. You have moved into acceptance and are deeply and profoundly sad. Your loss is palpable. The years are passing; your children are growing and you think of all the things your loved one is missing. You start to forget the sound of their voice.

Some days their death seems like a lifetime ago.

Before you know it, you hit the fourth year. You have it all down and you've become what my beau, Bryon, calls MAD. Mom and dad. You are doing it all and doing it quite well, actually. You and your children are used to being without your loved one. Sad but true. It's what we call, "the new norm" in my bereavement group.

By the fifth year, for many, you have met someone and you are trying to move forward. Notice how I said move forward, not move on, you will never truly move on. Moving forward into a new life. Not necessarily a worse life, just different. Different than you ever imagined, especially, in some cases, at such a young age.

THE FIVE STAGES – PART II

In this chapter, I am going to go through the stages again because I feel they are worth repeating as you will go through them time and time again.

Denial. I played tricks with myself when my loved ones died. When my dad passed away, I pretended he was visiting an exotic location, scouting the best coffee beans. When Jim died, as stated previously, I simply said to myself that he was on a business trip. When my mom died, I pretended she was at her condominium in Florida. It helped me cope, temporarily. Use or do whatever you need, to allow yourself to get through the day.

The beginning weeks and months are beyond hard. It's indescribable, so don't think one day at a time, think one hour at a time. There will even be some days when you need to think one minute at a time. If you don't think this way, the enormity of it will crush you and leave you immobile.

I can, however, tell you one thing I didn't do when I was in denial: I didn't drink. As a matter of fact, I didn't drink for months after Jim died. Family and friends were surprised. Not that I am a big boozer but I am known to like my wine, scotch or the occasional martini. It would have been so easy to drink, and frankly, given my situation, no one would have blamed me if I had.

Why would someone drink after losing a loved one? To dull the pain. To forget. I didn't drink, not because I knew alcohol is a depressant and something my late husband was also doing a lot of before he took his life. I didn't drink because I said, "I only drink when I'm happy" and clearly I was not happy.

Anger. Besides going to the cemetery and screaming, cursing at or even kicking my late husband's headstone, there were days when I was so mad at him that I would turn over all his pictures in our home because I couldn't stand to look at his smiling face. I also wouldn't call his mother because I didn't want to hear how wonderful he was.

What made me most angry at him was when my little girls would cry. That pain was unbearable. I could literally feel my heart break inside my chest. They would come home from school sad because the other children were making Father's Day cards for their dads or they had no one to take them to the Father/Daughter dance. Times like those I wanted to kill him again myself!

Someone told me to write a letter and say all the things I would like to say to him, then burn it. I did write a brief one, a year or so later and it helped a bit. But, large blocks of time, help from a therapist and my bereavement group, as well as a better understanding of the disease of depression were the only things that truly helped lessen my anger. Notice, ten years later I still say lessen. Perhaps, after ten years, I should write another letter. It's a process and there are no directions or rights or wrongs.

Bargaining. As I mentioned in my previous chapter, I will always wonder what would have happened if I had taken him to the psychiatric hospital the night he broke down in tears. He never mentioned suicide, nor would I ever in my wildest imagination have thought that he would do something like that to himself, to me, our girls, or his family. His best childhood friend, named Rich, hanged himself almost ten years earlier and Jim was so unbelievably mad at him. He just couldn't believe Rich would do that to his mother or to him. Jim could barely speak at his friend's funeral because he was shocked and so incredibly heartbroken.

Obviously, I knew my late husband was depressed but did I ever think for one minute he would kill himself? Not in a million years. In every picture I have of him, he is smiling the biggest, happiest grin you will ever see; it's so hard to comprehend how he masked his pain.

It was Jim's first and only suicide attempt. He used a shotgun so, to me, he wasn't just crying out for help. He wanted the job done; permanently. He had made up his mind. I found out months after he died that he was asking friends who were hunters if bullets ever expire. If I had known that; would I have seen it as a red flag? Would I have been able to save him? Would the right counselor or psychologist have been able to help him? I doubt it, but I guess I will never know. His best friend and neighbor, Paul, once said, "I guess I will find out why in forty years, God willing."

For the first year or two I beat myself up about it daily. I replayed it over and over in my mind. Unfortunately, again, time and understanding are the only things that helped me move forward from this step.

Depression. When my girls were at school, I would get depressed and restless, so I began signing myself up for all kinds of volunteer work. I became class mother for both my daughters, a PTA board member, a Girl Scout troop co-leader, and a special events coordinator for the YMCA. I also started cleaning my church, which I still do every Thursday. The idea is to keep moving at all costs. Move a muscle, change a thought. I also exercised, which is a great release.

I resumed my daily three-mile walks because I had to. I needed to feel the breath going in and out of my lungs to be present and aware.

There were, on some particularly bad days, times when I would have to sit on the curb and sob. I did anything and everything to keep myself moving. When you are active, you don't think as much or as deeply.

Acceptance. A very hard stage, especially with a suicide death. First I had PTSD, Post-Traumatic Stress Disorder. With the help of my friend, Valerie, (whom I had known for years and yet, ironically, never knew that she worked with suicide victims and their families), we were able to work through the shock. She sat me down shortly after Jim's death and made me describe, in total gory detail, everything I saw that horrific day. This helped me process what I saw. We then were able to replace some of the horror, like the shotgun, with better thoughts such as a bouquet of flowers. I know that sounds utterly ridiculous but it helped me cope, especially short term, as I was having nightmares or wasn't sleeping at all.

I also began to see a therapist for a year. This also helped me accept Jim's death, as my therapist's mother had chosen the same fate for herself. Additionally, my bereavement group was a tremendous help. Being with people who you have a commonality with was key to my healing process.

Finally, I truly believe that if it weren't for my strong faith, I would still be absolutely lost, ten years later.

GRIEF AND THE FIVE SENSES

It has been my experience that when you have had a significant loss, whether it be a spouse, a parent, a relative, or a friend, the next loss is even worse. It's because the losses are compounded. Not only are you grieving for the person you just lost, but you are grieving all over again for another loved one who died beforehand. In my opinion, I think it gets emotionally harder and harder with each loss. Why? You relive each one as if it just happened.

Going to a funeral home, any funeral home, after the loss of a loved one is difficult; however, going to the same funeral home is crippling. I remember having to go to my friend's father's wake shortly after my father was memorialized at the exact same funeral home. I sat in my car, chain smoking, trying to get the nerve to walk through the doors. When I was finally able to get myself inside, my legs literally buckled at the sight of the couch I sat on during my dad's two-day wake. I had to go back to that establishment twenty-five long years later to wake my beautiful mother and, I must say, it wasn't much easier, even after all that time.

The same held true when I had to go to a friend's wake at the place where Jim's wake took place. I was so anxious that I had to take half a Xanax so I could mourn a friend.

With each loss, there usually comes a wake and funeral. Each wake and funeral reminds you of others before it because so many things are similar, such as the flowers. Lilies are used quite a bit at funerals. They used to be one of my favorite flowers, but not anymore. Sometimes the mere smell of them brings me back to my late husband's wake.

My mom hated lilies; she used to say they reminded her of death, so instead, we used roses at her wake. Now I don't like roses anymore, especially as a gift, even on Valentine's Day.

Smell is a very powerful sense. When Jim died, I used to bury my nose in his shirts hanging in our walk-in closet. It was as if he were standing before me and, while sad, it strangely comforted me. If I am walking in my beloved New York City and get a whiff of my dad's cologne, who died over thirty years ago, I completely crumble. If my sister Laura wears my mom's favorite perfume, I immediately burst into tears.

Sound. Then, of course, there is music. Music always reminds one of certain people, places and moments in your life; it evokes a poignant memory. It is one of the many things I love about it. Most times, it can be a wonderful memory; however, sometimes it can bring you back to an exact moment in time, one that was incredibly sad.

A happy music memory is when I hear the Beatles, I think of my cousin, Billy. When I was young and we would go visit him in Brooklyn with my family and our other cousin, they would put on 45s and "I Want to Hold Your Hand" would play on a little record player and we would sing along. A sad memory, however, is every time I hear the Cars' song, "Drive," I always think of my dad's death to this day because it was on the radio right after I heard the news that he had died.

Of course, hymns are particularly difficult because they seem to play the same ones at every Catholic funeral mass. What makes it more upsetting is they also play them at Sunday mass quite a bit. "On Eagles' Wings," "I am the Bread of Life" and "Be Not Afraid" make me cry instantly. Because of the loss of my mom, "Ave Maria" is impossible for me to hear. When my daughters and I go to mass, they look up the hymns in the missal and, when they read it's one of "the big four," as I call them, they both say, "Oh no". They know that when they start one of those hymns, I will start sobbing, tears streaming down my face, reliving those awful days.

Taste. How can taste remind you of someone? My mom loved to shop and so did my sisters; however, I didn't inherit that gene, much to my two daughters' dismay. My mom and I would bond by going out to dinner. We were both big foodies, especially for our beloved French food. We had been to six out of ten of the top French restaurants in New York City as we were working our way through the list. While I still adore French food, I always think of my mom when I eat at a French restaurant and determine what she would eat and what she would think of the décor and the service. It can be sad, but it also makes me happy knowing she's smiling down on me, happy I am enjoying it and thinking of her.

Believe it or not touch can also make you think of a loved one. My mom was always cold and wore warm, cashmere sweaters. When I feel cashmere, I think of her immediately.

Sight. Seeing people who remind you of your loved one can be extremely difficult. When my dad died, seeing his brother, my uncle Bill, was so hard not only because he sounded so much like my dad and had the same hearty laugh, but he had my father's large Castellano eyes. It was heartbreaking being in his presence. Even though heartbreaking, I wanted to be around him regardless of how sad it made me. I wanted him to walk me down the aisle at my wedding because it would be so close to my having my dad there.

My Uncle Mike was my dad's youngest brother and even though he was my Godfather, I wanted to have my Uncle Bill do the honors but he died the year before I got married. Another major loss.

My former brother-in-law, Brian, reminds me so much of my late husband. You can definitely tell they are brothers; they look a lot alike. Additionally, they share all the same mannerisms. Sometimes, because they are so much alike, it's difficult to be around him. One of my daughters say it's creepy. We only see him once or twice a year so it's bearable; however, I wouldn't go out of my way to avoid him just because he reminds me of Jim.

While seeing and being with relatives that remind you of your loved one might be painful, it can also be like having them around again. It's all how you look at it.

One flower reminds you of one relative, another reminds you of another, so what do you do about your loved one's floral arrangement? There are hundreds of flower varieties to choose from so, while you don't want to use lilies because they remind you of another loved one's wake, choose either that person's favorite flower, if you know it, or perhaps one of their favorite colors.

While lilies and roses are very standard for wakes and funerals, ultimately it is your choice, so you don't have to stick to tradition and can choose whatever you want. Make it work for you.

NOW WHAT?

First, accept all help offered, especially in the beginning because people will eventually stop offering as time goes by. If no help is offered, swallow your pride and ask for help. I am a very strong, independent woman so asking for help is incredibly difficult. However, I am getting better at it and I must say, it's really a remarkable thing. People are usually very receptive but, for some reason, a number of them would rather you ask, unfortunately.

Your spouse has died, now what? Your mind is constantly spinning, so much so that sleep eludes you for days at a time. I have learned that the best thing to help with the "spinning wheel" is to make up two lists. The first one should be entitled, "Master List." On this list, write down everything that is keeping you up thinking at night. Keep a pad and pen with you at all times. I keep one in my bag, in my kitchen, in my car, and especially by my bed because that is usually when I have the most time to think. If your husband died, I am sure you are thinking about all the things he did in the house that will now become your responsibility. Who is going to cut the grass? Take out the trash? Shovel the driveway? Will I be able to stay in the house?

If it's your wife who's passed away, you are probably thinking about who is going to do the cooking? The laundry? Bake birthday cakes for my kids? The list is endless.

Next, write a "daily list." Put four or five things on it and try, notice how I said try, to get at least two things (notice how I didn't say all) accomplished. Whatever you didn't get around to that day should get carried over to tomorrow's list. Jim died ten years ago and I still do my lists.

So, you've taken on his chores in addition to your own. Now what? Do you have a lawn mower? Do you know how to run it? If so, do you have the time to do it or, if you don't have the time, do you have the money to hire someone? The same holds true for shoveling the driveway.

Now, with me, we didn't own a push mower; we had a small tractor that I had no idea how to run nor did I want to learn.

My girls were little when my husband died and one of their favorite memories was their dad driving them around the lawn on the tractor. They loved it. My youngest daughter actually had a barnyard-themed second birthday party and my husband drove the kids around our yard. Obviously, besides me not knowing how to work the tractor, their memories were happy so I just couldn't do it. I wouldn't do it. It was what they did together. Frankly, it just wouldn't be the same. Then again, nothing will ever be the same.

I did, however, ask my neighbor, my husband's best friend, Paul, to show me how to work various other power tools such as the leaf blower, pressure washer and especially our generator and snow blower. I took notes on each piece of equipment, writing the steps in order of operation, and tacked them to the bulletin board I had in my garage. If you have a garage, you might want to buy one and hang it. I must say, it came in very handy.

I also have a list of every one of our utility companies' phone numbers, local repair shops and other important numbers hanging on that board for easy reference. I still refer to it. It's amazing the things you can do if your back is against the wall and you literally have no other choice. I snow blow my entire driveway, all 157 feet of it, every winter, myself, all winter long. Me, the spoiled brat. However, what is the alternative? Pay someone $65 - $75 for each snow fall over three inches? With the winters we have been having lately, I would be in the poor house in no time.

For the past ten years I've found myself doing all sorts of things I never would have attempted if my husband hadn't passed away. This spring, I plan on tackling my next project. I am going to attempt to power wash my front porch and back deck, then stain both myself. Wish me luck.

Beside the chores, worse, for me, has been managing the finances. My daughters will tell you, I am far from a math whiz. If the truth be told, I haven't been able to help them with their math homework since third grade. If you are lucky enough to have a bit of insurance or inheritance money, I would highly recommend that you hire a financial advisor. My dear friend Amy told me about her mom's financial professional, and I am so grateful to this day. She has done a remarkable job and I feel confident about my retirement years.

Thankfully, my girls and I were eligible for Social Security. Income coming in meant I didn't have to find a job immediately. Because the girls were so young, I wanted to be home for them. Check with your Social Security office to see if you're eligible for survivor benefits.

Additionally, my late husband had life insurance. I hope your spouse was able to provide you with this gift. If you don't already know, child care is quite expensive; it almost doesn't pay to get a full-time job. If you earn over some puny amount of income, the government will take away your Social Security benefits. Another thing no one tells you.

Here is something you don't want to live without: an alarm system. First of all, people now know you are a widow/widower. To me, that means you are a target. I hardly slept in the beginning, but once I got an alarm system installed, I started sleeping through the night. It is very reassuring to come home and see the armed light on. You know there wasn't someone in your home or worse, still in your home.

Before the alarm, I used to check the whole house when we would come home from somewhere, worried someone was hiding in my home ready to pounce at any given moment. At night, I loved seeing the armed button light up again because if I heard a noise in the middle of the night, as one often does with a thirty-year-old home, I would know it was just that: a noise. Having an alarm system will give you peace of mind. They might be a little expensive, but well worth it.

One less thing to worry about.

BEST PIECE OF ADVICE

There were so many similarities between me and my mother. First, we both enjoyed cooking and entertaining. We cleaned certain rooms of our homes on certain days. We were librarians in our children's schools. We both volunteered to clean our churches. We both quit smoking at approximately the same age and in a very similar manner. The list goes on and on.

However, of all our similarities, I never thought there would be one we shared that was painful and terribly sad. My mom and I were both young widows. I was 42 when Jim suddenly passed away by committing suicide. My mom was 51 when my dad died of a massive heart attack on his way home from the hospital.

My mother was at our family condominium in Madeira Beach, Florida, when I called her, incoherent with my unimaginable news on that beautiful spring day. She answered on the third ring and all I could squeak out was, "Mom".

Being a mother, her mom instincts kicked in and she immediately said, "What's the matter?" Again, all I could croak was, "Mom."

She again asked me what was wrong. I said it again, one more time, "Mom" then blurted the horrible line, "Jim blew his head off." She couldn't understand me as I said the line very fast. I repeated it several more times but too fast for her to understand my rush of words, or perhaps she did hear me but simple didn't want to. She told me to slow down, that she couldn't understand me, so I said the horrible line again only slower. She finally heard me, understood and was speechless and thoroughly wounded, like any mother would be with that kind of news from her daughter. I know if one of my daughters called with that news, my heart would literally break in half for her and her children. My mom didn't have much to say after that and I understood. What could she possibly say?

My mom did not like to fly, plus she had CREST Syndrome, which is a form of scleroderma, and a mild heart condition. My siblings and even friends and relatives offered to fly down and accompany her back home to New York; however, she ultimately made the decision not to fly home in order to attend my husband's wake and funeral.

While most people were shocked, to say the least, I was happy. Happy she wasn't going to see her little girl an inconsolable mess. My mother-in-law was not happy. However, I didn't hear her verbalize it until seven years after her son's death.

I can't and don't blame my mom for not coming. I recently found out from her childhood friend, Carol, who she grew up in Brooklyn with that she was incredibly angry at my husband and, frankly, she had every right to be. I know if someone left my baby alone to raise two little girls, I'd be furious too. Additionally, my mother was not one to show her emotions, especially in public. My sister and I called her the "Jackie O Widow".

Not only did my mom have all the above-mentioned conditions and reasons for not coming, what I didn't know, and she didn't either at the time, was that she had cancer and would die fourteen short months after my husband. To this day, I am convinced my father's death and my husband's caused or certainly contributed to her getting lung and colon cancers. If you believe in homeopathy as I do, lungs are about grief and the colon is about letting go.

Three weeks after Jim took his life, my girls and I flew down to Florida. We were supposed to fly down as a family; the tickets were bought several months earlier. It was our traditional spring break trip. Not only did I want to go, I thought it would be good for us to get away as we were in the spotlight 24/7 since everyone knew our story. Plus, I needed to see and hug my mom.

Before coming down, my mom told my brother and sisters that she was nervous, that she didn't know what to say to me. I have to admit, I was nervous too. I didn't know what to expect or how she would react. When we walked in, she hugged her granddaughters fiercely and told them she was sorry and that she loved them. Plain and simple. That alone nearly killed me because I could see how incredibly painful it was for her to say that to them. It was truly heartbreaking. Then she looked at me, with pure sadness and horror. I wasn't a pretty sight. I had lost 12 pounds and was down to 114. I looked like a walking skeleton. My clothes were hanging off me and my face looked old, tired, worn. She hugged me and we both cried for a bit wrapped in each other's arms; however, deep down inside I knew she was mad at Jim. A stage of grief I wasn't anywhere near.

On the first night that we were there, long after my girls had gone to bed, my mother decided to impart some advice to me. This was rare for my mother as she was a very private person who, as I mentioned, held her emotions and thoughts in check. She said, "Don't wait too long to get remarried because you're going to get used to it."

I had just lost my husband and I thought, "What a terrible thing to say to me. Why on earth would she say something like that? Get used to what?" For years after she said that, I would hear her words echoing in my head not fully understanding their meaning.

I have been without my husband for ten years now, and I must admit, I'm used to it just being me and my girls, sad to say. I am used to taking out the garbage, paying the bills, taking in the mail and even shoveling the driveway. All his chores. Besides that, I am now at the point where I can't fathom having to share my space, never mind my closet or, God forbid, my bathroom with someone else again. I can't imagine having someone other than myself to decide on things, from the very small, like what to have for dinner, to where to go on vacation, to the very large, like whether to refinance the mortgage or what car to buy next.

I have always been a strong woman but grew even stronger after my dad died, and then even more so after the deaths of my husband and mother. I have come to rely on no one but myself. I am totally self-sufficient. I am doing my chores and his and, I must admit, I'm damn good at both. While I have dated over the past eight years, I have yet to find a man stronger than myself, that is, until I met Bryon last year.

Unfortunately, I have been both man and woman for so long that I don't know how to just be the woman or let someone in fully. These concepts have been so foreign to me for so long; however, since I have found the right man I am willing to at least give it a try.

Perhaps your spouse was **a** love in your life but maybe not **the** love of your life. When you are ready, go out, meet people, take a chance because who knows what the future might hold?

Perhaps my mother was right, since I am not remarried and I am now very used to being alone. I guess, once again, maybe I should have listened to my mother.

THE HARDEST DAY OF MY LIFE

I thought the hardest day of my life would be telling my two girls that their daddy died. Don't get me wrong, that was so unbelievably hard, heartbreaking actually. But worse, way worse, was telling them HOW he died.

The police, EMS and curious on-lookers had finally departed; even the coroner was gone. It was after 4:00 p.m. and I had just been to the local hospital with my brother at the insistence of my doctor and was checked out both physically and emotionally, by my doctor and a clinical psychologist on staff. I barely remember it. The only thing I truly remember was that I kept looking down at my gardening shoes; I kept staring at how they were falling apart. I sat at a desk in a conference room and answered all their questions, albeit slowly and in a monotone voice. It was obvious to my doctor and the psychologist that I was suffering from PTSD: Post-Traumatic Stress Disorder. After an hour of questions, they deemed I was competent enough to take care of myself and my daughters, so I was given a prescription for Xanax and sent home.

When I got home, late that afternoon, I knew I couldn't put it off any longer. It was time to face my daughters and tell them the terrible news. How do you tell your children, ages seven and four-and-a-half, that their daddy died and was never coming home? I tried to think of what I would say on the short ride home from the hospital but no words came to me. I decided at that moment that I wasn't going to rehearse what I said, I obviously couldn't, so whatever came out of my head and heart was going to have to do.

It was now well after 5:00 p.m. and both my daughters were at my neighbor, Juliette's house. I will always be thankful that they were there, and not at our home when I told them, because somehow it made it a bit easier. I didn't want them to have that memory in our home.

I know that might sound ridiculous, but when someone tells you that kind of horrific news, you will remember it for the rest of your life. You will remember the details of that day—who told you, how they told you, where you were, what kind of day it was. Every detail will be etched in your brain *forever*. So, if you are the one breaking that kind of heartbreaking news, be mindful of what you say, how you say it, and your surroundings because they matter.

When I got to Juliette's, our girls were downstairs on the couch together watching television. You could tell they were confused. All I kept thinking was, "God, give me strength." I sat down on a coffee table across from the couch where they were sitting. I didn't sugar coat it, I simply blurted out, "Daddy died today." They didn't say too much. They both just hugged me, buried their little heads in my lap and cried and cried until they couldn't cry anymore.

My brother Peter, and my sister Laura, were there for support. Frankly, I don't remember much, if anything, of what I said to them other than the fact that he was in Heaven and he had to leave us but would watch over them and would always be with them.

According to my brother, I said even more. My brother said it was perfect. God must have given me the words. After they were done crying, I took them home where they climbed into their beds and went to sleep. I fully expected one if not both of them to want to sleep with me, not that they ever did, but they didn't ask. They didn't ask questions such as how he died or was he in an accident. Nothing. They just accepted the fact that their daddy was gone with pure sadness.

The suddenness of his death left us all in such deep shock and shook me to my very core.

The next day, Friday, my girls got up, ate breakfast, played with their toys and spent the day like they normally did; their routine unchanged. The only thing different about that day was they didn't go to school. I even drove them, how, I don't know, to an Easter party on Saturday. I remember pulling over at the reservoir near my house after dropping them off and screaming, "Why?" over and over at the top of my lungs and banging my hands on the steering wheel until my palms were sore. I went home, washed my face and went back to pick them up as if nothing had transpired. When they got home, they acted the way they always did, like two ordinary little girls.

After the heartbreaking wake on Sunday and the even sadder funeral on Monday, one day led into another. Before I knew it, weeks had passed. Their lives picked up where they left off. I, on the other hand, was on autopilot, doing things by rote. I was, however, feeling weighed down by their not knowing how he died. I felt I was harboring a deep, dark secret. I knew I had to tell them, not because that's what the school psychologist or other so-called experts said, I just knew in my heart of hearts that it would inevitably be the best thing I could do for them, for us. I just didn't know how. I did know, however, that when the moment was right the opportunity would present itself. Approximately three agonizing months passed before God gave me that opportunity.

It was a bright, sunny day in June at approximately 2:30 in the afternoon. My daughters had just come home from a birthday party and were in a good mood. We were sitting in our family room, the sun streaming through the skylight, and I knew at that exact moment that it was the right time.

"Alexandra, do you know how Daddy died?"

She said, "Yes, he was in a car accident."

I said, "Who told you that?"

She replied, "A friend at school."

To which I replied, "Well, that's not true. I never told you how he died because I have been waiting for you to ask me but you never did."

So, she said, "Then how did he die?"

I took a deep breath and replied, "He committed suicide."

Having just turned seven she of course said, "What's suicide?"

I replied, "It is when you take your own life."

She hesitated a moment, then my very intelligent little girl said, "He was like Jesus, he sacrificed his life for us."

I was utterly speechless. Her next question was, of course, "Why?" I replied, "Daddy was sick. He had something called depression and should have gone to a doctor to take care of his himself like when you go to the doctor when you are sick."

Then she said, "How?"

I replied, "You remember the shotguns Grandpa gave Daddy that Mommy didn't like in the house? He used one of those and shot himself."

Then came the word, "Where?"

To which I replied, "His workshop."

At this point, my four-and-a-half-year-old daughter hadn't said a word; she just sat there listening. The first and only thing she said was, "I'm confused Mama, who shot him?"

Once the secret was out, I knew we would start the healing process. I felt an incredible weight and terrible secret had been lifted from my shoulders. As painful as this day was, I came to find out through my bereavement center that telling them, even though they were incredibly young, was the best thing I could have possibly done. Some people in our bereavement group didn't tell their children the truth when their parent committed suicide. They lied to them, thinking it would be easier on their children, because they just wouldn't understand. They were told the parent died in a car accident or had a heart attack.

For many years these children grew up thinking that's how their parent died, only to be told the truth or, worse, find out the truth on their own. Once they discovered they were lied to, these children felt ultimately betrayed and had to grieve all over again. Many of these children began to self-medicate to ease the pain.

My advice is to be honest with your children, no matter how young. Children should be told the truth, no matter how difficult it is or whether you think they are mature enough to comprehend. As we went through this tragedy, I learned that children are resilient. Give them the benefit of the doubt and be open and honest with them because, if not, the repercussions later on will be tenfold.

DADDY'S LITTLE GIRL

I grew up in a lovely suburban town called New City, New York, which is about forty miles north of Manhattan. It was and still is a wonderful place to raise a family.

When my parents moved there over fifty years ago, it was very rural, so much so that there were more deer than cars. When I was young, my brother Peter, my sisters, Laura and Karen and I had a wonderful life. There were 46 kids on our block so there was always someone to play with at any given time of day. We played all the usual games: kickball, whiffle ball, basketball, and flashlight tag. We rode our bikes until our legs couldn't pedal anymore. We explored the sewer system and caught crayfish in the brook.

In the winter, we skated on Greenburg's pond behind my house, went sleigh riding or built snow forts and had snowball fights. The summers seemed endless and the winters were snowy wonderlands. It was a magical place when I was a young child; however, when I became a teenager, I got bored with my surroundings and used to say our town was for the newly wed or nearly dead.

I was the youngest of four children. Because of where I fell in the pecking order, my siblings named me DLG, short for Daddy's Little Girl. I could do no wrong in my father's eyes and my brother and sisters knew it. If we were together, and they were teasing me, or if I just wanted to get them in trouble, all I would have to yell was, "Daddy!" and everyone, except me of course, would be punished.

My dad, Peter, or Pete as he was called, was an amazing, self-made man. After my father got out of the Marines, he got a job in the mail room of Savarin coffee. He absorbed as much as he could about the coffee business while he was there, then left to take a position in the coffee tasting program at Nestles. He knew his trade so well that he was interviewed for his coffee tasting skills by Joan Lunden when she was a young, twenty-something reporter. He also was interviewed for Delta's in-flight magazine.

My dad worked his way up the corporate ladder over the years and eventually became senior manager of coffee purchasing. If my dad had gone to college, as he wanted to, he would have become a vice president and was even told that by his boss. Unfortunately, instead of college, he had to work at his parents' bar in Brooklyn.

Dad and I were pretty close when I was young. I say pretty close because he left the house at 5:00 a.m. every day to beat the traffic over the Tappan Zee Bridge. He hated traffic.

When he got home, at 5:00, he would walk into our kitchen, undo his tie, and give my mom a kiss while she was cooking dinner. He occasionally had to wine and dine clients at lunch so he rarely, if ever, had a cocktail when he got home, even though that was pretty much the norm of that generation. Maybe that's why he and my mom looked forward to their Saturday night date.

He would then go up to their bedroom, change out of his suit and we would have dinner, 5:30 p.m. sharp. After he ate, he relaxed by watching television before retiring for the night. I fell asleep every night to "The Honeymooners" theme.

My earliest memory is of my dad lying on our thick gold colored living room carpet and me sitting on his chest tickling him and him tickling me; I couldn't have been more than three.

Every Sunday, after mass, he would make me a big delicious egg breakfast complete with fried Italian cold cuts such as salami and pepperoni. He would serve it with hunks of fresh Italian bread covered in butter.

We would go to flea markets together on Saturdays, which were held at the local drive-in. He would buy everyone in the family, and even sometimes your friends or boyfriends, gifts or clothes as he had impeccable taste and was incredibly generous.

Occasionally, on Sundays, we would hit a tennis ball as we had a court for the winter at a local tennis club. When I was little, he would mail me postcards when he traveled around the world buying coffee beans for Nestles. Occasionally, my dad would buy me small gifts from the exotic places he visited. I treasured them all and still have the postcards and a trinket or two.

My favorite memories were when we would watch our two favorite movies together; "The Wizard of Oz" when I was small and, as I got older, "Young Frankenstein." He was my protector when we watched "The Wizard of Oz" as I would hide behind him every time I caught a glimpse of the wicked witch or the flying monkeys. Every time the cowardly lion came on, he would roar with laughter.

As I got older, and we watched the blind man scene in "Young Frankenstein," Gene Hackman would cause him to laugh so hard his eyes would glisten with tears.

My dad had a wonderful deep laugh. During my senior year of high school, my father got sick and ended up in the hospital, unable to attend my High School graduation. I was completely devastated. The doctors thought it was very bad indigestion and stress. However, little did we know at the time, that he was having a series of small heart attacks.

The next year, the year I finished business school, he bought a one-bedroom apartment on the Upper West Side in New York City in a lovely one-hundred-year-old brownstone. My oldest sister, Karen, and I moved in. My father had to be convinced to buy it because, at the time, the block wasn't very safe. It had two burnt out buildings on the corner and was known as "glassine alley" from all the empty glassine drug bags littering the street.

My sister used to rent an apartment with a girlfriend in the building on the third floor facing the street which is how she learned the building was going co-op. She told my dad it would be a wonderful investment and encouraged him to buy it. My father had one stipulation: I had to move in with my sister as he didn't want her living alone.

I had no intention of living in New York City; I loved visiting but I did not want to live there. After much thought, however, I decided to give it a try for one year. I kept telling myself that it's a good place to start and, if I could make it there, I could make it anywhere. Ah, good old Sinatra logic.

I was in the city several weeks pounding the pavement going on multiple interviews until I landed my first job as a junior secretary working at SCM Corporation. My first job ever! Being a DLG (remember: Daddy's Little Girl) had its advantages. Growing up, I never had a job other than the occasional babysitting gig. I would spend my summers floating around our beautiful 20' x 40' in-ground pool or doing chores around our house. Basically, my dad would finance my summer fun by palming me money as I walked out the door; he would keep it on the QT so my mother wouldn't find out. I'll admit it, I was spoiled rotten.

I called my dad, for free, from my office quite often to talk about my job. He genuinely seemed interested in me and my life. Suddenly, we seemed to have more things to talk about and we were getting even closer. Daddy's little girl once again.

The following summer, despite it being a hot, steamy August day, I was in a great mood strolling through Central Park on my way home from work. I was wearing one of my favorite, brightly-color sleeveless sheath dresses with sneakers, having ditched my spike heels for my three-mile trek home. Why was I in a great mood? My dad was being released from the hospital after being in the ICU for over a week. It was a Monday and I had just seen my dad the day before, Sunday, before heading back into the City. I had visited him at the hospital both days that weekend. Not only did I want to see him, but I wanted to bring him some of my mother's spaghetti. He was not fond of the hospital food, but, frankly who is?

We would bring him my mom's delicious home cooking every chance we got. I knew he wasn't well that Sunday because he didn't dig in the minute I gave it to him like he usually did; he told me to set it aside.

Then, I said to him, "Dad, you should call your brothers and sisters and tell them you are in the hospital."

He said, "Why? When it's my time, it's my time and they will understand." As I was leaving, I kissed my dad on the cheek and said goodbye. The words, "I love you" were stuck in my throat. I couldn't get those words out because I knew my dad would just brush them off as he always did. He, and his generation, had a hard time expressing emotions. I will never forgive myself for not saying those three little words that day!

When you are young, you never think anything bad is going to happen, especially to your parents, that is, unless they are old. So the thought never entered my head that when I said goodbye that Sunday afternoon, it would be the last time I would see my dad.

On a muggy Monday evening, August 27, 1984, I got the phone call from my sister Laura that shattered my world and forever changed my life. That was the first time, notice I said first time, that I truly understood the meaning of the term, broken heart. I literally felt mine break in half that day. Upon hearing the news, I let out a blood-curdling scream and ran out of our apartment and into the street thinking I could stop my sister Karen from taking off to Riverdale to see her boyfriend Marco. She had left at least a half hour earlier. Why did I think I would be able to stop her? Suddenly, nothing made sense in my world.

My dad died on his way home from the hospital. My sister had gone to pick him up and he asked her to drive. Right then and there it should have been a red flag that he wasn't well as my dad loved to drive. Plus, he hated to be driven. Not long after they left the hospital, he suffered a massive heart attack.

My sister pulled over and gave him mouth to mouth. His final words were, "Take care of your mother." And with those words he was gone. My world has never been the same, even after all these years. My rock, the first man in my life, my idol, my hero was gone.

Now it breaks my heart all over again when I think about my two girls. How they grew up without a dad. How they haven't been able to utter the word daddy in ten long years. How, like me, their dad won't be there to walk them down the aisle at their wedding or hold his first grandchild.

I must admit, all these years later, I wonder how different they might be if they'd grown up with a father instead of just me trying to be both. Since my late husband was the calm one, would they be more like him, easy going and even-tempered, and less like me, their explosive, emotional, hot headed all-Italian mom? Would they be better in math? Sports? Would they know how to fix things? Change a tire?

I remember teaching Alexandra how to drive. I was impatient and frightened and when I am frightened, I yell. Not something you should do with a young, first-time driver. Jim was a car guy; he adored everything about them and was very patient. He would have been so much better at this than me. I guess I will always wonder how they could be different. However, the thing I am saddest about is how they missed out on being called Daddy's little girls.

BEREAVEMENT GROUP:

THE GROUP NO ONE WANTS TO BELONG TO

When my husband died, several people suggested that I attend a bereavement group. If you don't think you need this type of support, think again. I can tell you first hand that you need the support of other people going through what you experience. Your friends will be supportive and say they understand what you're going through, but they really have no idea if they haven't been through the same thing. Unless they have walked a mile in your grief-ridden shoes, they haven't a clue.

I really didn't want to go, as I am a pretty private person and I certainly did not want to tell my story - our story - to complete strangers. I decided to go for my children's sake. It was ironic because, in the end, I was the one who cried and had a hard time saying goodbye to our group.

There are many types of bereavement groups. Some are offered through your local hospital, hospice, or by your place of worship. Some deal with the loss of a spouse while others deal with the loss of a child. I knew I did not want to go to a bereavement group and find that everyone there was sixty-five and over. I wanted to find a group with widows/widowers close to my age as I needed a common bond with people who could relate to my specific situation.

All bereavement groups have different sets of rules. Someone, I am not exactly sure who, since, as I mentioned, the first several months were a blur, suggested this particular group that worked with families, especially young families. Being a young widow of 42, I thought it sounded like a good fit.

The one we eventually chose suggested that we wait for three months before joining. I thought that was odd because we needed their help immediately, but those were the rules and there obviously must have been a reason. In the meantime, I thought it was important to get help for my girls because they were so young and I knew they were having a hard time wrapping their heads around their dad's death. If I couldn't understand it, how on earth could they?

Again, I don't remember who suggested it, but I decided to hire an art therapist.

I found a lovely woman who came to our home once a week. Art turned out to be a perfect medium for my children. It is truly a wonderful way to help young children understand their grief, especially if they are having a hard time expressing it verbally. I highly recommend it.

When we were finally able to join the bereavement group we selected, after the three-month waiting period, I knew right away that my girls and I were in the right place. The doors to the local Methodist church opened a half hour before group started. Pizza, salad, non-caffeinated soda, coffee and cookies were served in the common room. Pizza is a perfect little meal for anyone but certainly ideal for children.

We sat alone for the first several weeks until we got to know some regulars. Then we began to sit and chat with other families before being split into our groups. My girls were separated from each other, which worried me in the beginning, but I understood why; they sorted the children's groups by age. Things began to make sense.

After our pizza dinner, the program chairperson asked if an individual from each family would stand, state their names, who they lost and how they died. I was horrified. I couldn't do it. So, my very brave seven-year-old said she would represent our family. One by one, families stood to introduce themselves and tell their stories. Each was so incredibly sad.

Next, it was my daughter's turn. We heard her say, "I'm Alexandra. This is my sister Samantha and my mom, Kim. We lost my dad, her husband, Jim, to suicide, March 30, 2006.

This was beyond heartbreaking, but I knew we were in the right place as it was the first time I heard my daughter verbalize our story. The healing for what was left of our family began in that room on that day.

I cannot stress enough the importance of finding a bereavement group that is right for you. I tried one myself which was specifically for people who'd lost someone to suicide, but I didn't form an immediate bond with anyone there. All of their spouses or children had either attempted suicide before or were bi-polar and, more than likely, off their meds. I couldn't relate, as my late husband was seemingly the happiest person I or anyone around him knew. He didn't fit the bill, so

I wasn't happy in this particular group. I encourage you to keep trying until you find a group that fits.

The group we found for our family was amazing. As I mentioned, the children were separated by age and placed in groups with two counselors. I, on the other hand, was placed in a group with bereaved widows and widowers and parents whose children had died, until the program chair decided that those who had lost children needed a group of their own, as their grief was very different in many ways than ours. When I walked in and sat down at the conference table, I looked at all the grief-etched faces. What a sad awakening to see so many young widows and widowers in one room!

When you think you have a sad story, think again, as someone else's is definitely sadder than yours. Hard to believe but true. I know it shouldn't make you feel better but, sorry to say, it does somehow.

We had a facilitator who ran the group. She also was a widow. She would have us go around the room and speak about whatever topic she happened to bring up that day. Some days we didn't always stick to the topic. In that hour, we talked about our loved ones who passed away. Sometimes, one or several people would cry. The tissue box was continually passed around the room. Occasionally, we got parenting tips from each other or social security information but mostly we shared our experiences, our strength and eventually our hopes.

Seeing these people week after week was comforting to me. I was enjoying their company. I formed bonds with several people. Some are

Facebook friends, others have become close friends and we get together for dinner a few times a year to this day.

My girls thrived there. They were able to speak freely about their dad and not be judged. It was not like life at school where they never spoke of him for fear of being a freak; the odd kid with one parent. This group of kids were just like them; they got it.

If they wanted to speak in their group, just like in the adult group, they would say what was on their minds when it was their turn. If they didn't want to share, they could simply say, "I pass" and they would not have to speak that particular day.

My girls made memory boxes and other arts and crafts, but the most memorable objects were something they called memory pillows. They were asked to bring in a picture of themselves with their dad. Next, they were taught how to sew a pocket in the back of the pillow, which they could fill with small trinkets reminding them of their dad. Once the picture was transposed on to the pillow, they got to write on it and decorate it.

It was a wonderful project that they looked forward to doing every year. Since we were there for a few years, they each have three memory pillows of my late husband which they keep in their rooms to this day.

When the evening was over, we would all pile back into the common room. The program director would have us all form a circle and hold hands. She would ask who had a birthday coming up and, once someone was identified, the director would ask that person to start "the squeeze". You would squeeze the person's hand next to you and the squeeze, kind of like the wave, would go all around the room. The kids especially thought it was a neat way to end the evening.

The third year we came back after summer recess, they placed all of the newly bereaved with us "old timers" as we used to call ourselves. We were all so distraught after the first fall session that we spoke to the program director and asked her if she could break the newbies off into their own group. Their grief was so new, so raw, that it set us all back to when it had just happened to us.

Because we had made such progress, no one wanted to go back there. We were in shock that we had once been like them; shells of people who were barely able to speak.

How far we had come. So, again, if you don't think bereavement groups are for you, I strongly encourage you to think again. I sincerely doubt that you and your family will regret it.

DOWN ONE PARENT

Your spouse has died. You are now a one-parent home. You are both mother and father.

Down one parent.

On our second date, my beau, Bryon said to me, "You're MAD."

I said, "Excuse me?" In my head I am thinking *he doesn't know me well enough to say that.* He laughed when he saw the shocked look on my face and replied, "You're MAD. You are both mom and dad."

"Wow, I never thought of it that way," I mumbled in awe. Yes, unfortunately that is exactly what I am. MAD, in every sense of the word.

What does it mean to be MAD, mom and dad? Where do I begin! First, when you are in a one-parent home, there is no playing good cop versus bad cop. You are both good and bad cop and you have absolutely no back up! This makes it impossible when trying to negotiate with children without an alternative solution provider.

How many times did you say no to your child on a particular subject, whether it was staying up late or wanting a particularly expensive toy? What did they usually do? They would run screaming to the other parent, pleading their case. Not anymore. No now means no. Plain and simple. There's no going to the other parent to try and get them on your side or to have them reason with the other parent. There is no other parent. Not only does this create havoc for the remaining parent but it also negates other choices for the children.

Being the only parent is different than being a single parent, way different. First of all, nine times out of ten, if you are separated or divorced, you are still in contact with your child's other parent. You often have back up. Maybe not exactly when a negotiation is in progress but certainly the next day. Your children still have two parents to play off of and they will, if you give them the chance. Remember, you have to stay strong, stick to your guns because, most times, they outnumber you.

My dear friend, Amy, was a single mom and I was always in awe of how she juggled work, day care, and her life in general. I watched with admiration as she raised Daniel all through our twenties and thirties. I watched him grow from a truly wonderful, polite, well-mannered little boy to the incredible twenty-eight-year-old man he has become. Raising my girls by myself for the past ten years, I can truly appreciate it even more.

As I mention in the chapter titled, 'Plenty of Frogs,' dating a widow/widower is way different, with so many more complications. In addition to having your children 24/7, 365 days of the year, unlike if you were divorced, you have to deal with the simple fact that your children are thinking that you are trying to replace the person you lost. Not true but, unfortunately, that's exactly where their minds go.

There is no divide and conquer. What does that mean? Well, let's say you are at an amusement park and the line is extremely long, there is only you now. That means you have to stand with your children on the long line, waiting. There is no other parent to come and take the kids to play a game, buy them a cool drink or even take them to the rest room. This is even worse for someone like me who is absolutely terrified of rides and has to leave her children unattended on the ride and wait for them at a different place than where I dropped them off.

That's especially terrifying in today's world.

How about open house at school? My girls are two years, five months apart so they are in the same school at least one year which makes open house night hell. You have to decide which teachers to meet of which child. How do you decide? It's a crap shoot; you basically roll the dice.

When your children are young, you have to deal with the Mother's Day/Father's Day dilemma. How do you acknowledge the day? When my girls were young, they would come home in tears because all the kids in their class made Father's Day cards. They inevitably ended up making them too but would put them in plastic bags to ward against the elements and would bring them to the cemetery with heavy hearts. Now that my girls are teenagers and I always comment how I am MAD, I teased them this past Father's Day and asked them where my cards and gifts were. They took me seriously and felt bad, momentarily, that they didn't buy me anything. I was only kidding; well, sort of.

How do you deal with Father/Daughter dances when you have lost your husband? Why do they do this ritual at school? It is not necessary.

It is as bad as the Father/Daughter Mother/Son dance at a wedding. Both are incredibly heartbreaking for those who have lost a parent, or two!

Here is another huge dilemma. I am obviously a woman who has two daughters, so talking to my daughters about their periods was a no-brainer; however, what if you are a man left to raise a daughter, or two? How do you handle this subject?

How about going about purchasing their first bra? Of course, the same holds true in reverse. What if you are a woman raising a son? Who is going to tell them about spontaneous erections? Who is going to teach them to pee standing up? To throw a football? Defend themselves? Shave? Hopefully you have a sister, brother or close friend who can step in and help, but more than likely you will stumble through the best you can all by yourself.

How do you get used to filling out paperwork for your child's school or other institutions and being faced over and over again with questions about your spouse's information? Do you write 'deceased' in the blank next to their name or simply draw a line through it? I still to this day, ten years later, write 'deceased' because I want people to know that I am neither divorced nor a single woman with a child. It is important that I mention him so others know he existed and I do it now so people know that, while he is physically gone, he is always going to be part of my life in some way, shape or form.

It's good to write that you are a widow or widower so you get the benefit of using the widow's/widower's card when you need it. (See

'Widow's/Widower's Card' chapter.) I can tell you from experience that it is not fun to be by yourself, whether it's at a family gathering or a school event. Unfortunately, there will be lots of them. It is the worst in the beginning; all you can think of is that they should be there. Then, after a year or so has passed, you think about how much they are missing.

Eight years after my husband died, I was at my daughter's confirmation. The parents were asked to stand up and I was the only single person standing. I literally could feel the stares. Over the years you learn to ignore it, to stare straight ahead and remember the day isn't about you, it is about your child and they should be the focus of your thoughts.

By far, the worst part of being an only parent is when you are sick. This is when the children get truly scared, especially if your spouse got ill and passed away. They immediately think that is what is going to happen to you and that they will end up with no parents. Then what? They immediately think about what is going to happen to them. Heartbreaking.

Like I discussed in my chapter, 'Wills and Whatnot', make sure you have a guardian designated for your children and let them know who that person is and what the game plan is, should God forbid, that day ever come. My daughter, Alexandra, said once when I was very sick with the flu, "I know, I know, if anything happens to you, we go to Aunt Laura and live in New Jersey." So incredibly sad for me to hear but happy nonetheless that the fear of the unknown was gone!

Remember, there are no rules. Do the best job you can do. Some days will be far harder than others, but take the good with the bad and enjoy them anyway, because that is all you can do.

THE EFFECTS OF ALCOHOL

My late husband's father was an alcoholic. I heard the stories long after Jim and I met. Later on in our marriage, I got to witness an episode or two. Jim grew up in an environment that was totally foreign to me. His father was a very critical and verbally abusive man, unlike my dad. I hate to admit it, but I despised him. He never had anything good to say, ever. If it was a sunny day and I commented how lovely it was, he would find something negative to say.

Secretly, I used to call him "Doom and Gloom" or "Doctor Dread."

When Jim's parents divorced after twenty-four years of marriage, the emotional damage to my late husband was already done. Jim was in college when his parents finally split up. However, when he would come home, he would stay with his father. I don't know why. His mother is the polar opposite of her ex-husband. She is a bubbly woman who praises her children daily and loves them unconditionally.

My late husband was a kind, compassionate, honest man who could talk to anyone. If you were at a party or a function and didn't know a soul, he would sense that you were uncomfortable and would befriend you for the night, so that you would relax a bit and perhaps even enjoy your evening. He was a master at putting people at ease. He also liked to fix things—anything, and was incredibly handy, but I think he especially enjoyed trying to fix broken people.

He would chat up a homeless person in New York City in a heartbeat. So, it did not surprise me in the least when I heard the story and found out he would visit his alcoholic father often. So, in essence, my husband took on the role of caretaker. I actually think he thought he could save his father.

Over the next few years, this man "poisoned" his son. He would point out all his flaws on a daily basis. My former father-in-law was obsessively supercritical. In the years that we were married, I don't think I ever heard a good or kind word come out of his mouth except, perhaps, when Alexandra, his first grandchild was born. No matter how much my husband accomplished in his life or all the renovations he did to our home, or how much he sought his father's praise, he never got it, certainly not ever in my presence. He died seeking his father's love and approval.

I met Jim where many people did when they were young and single – at a bar. It wasn't an upscale or even ordinary bar; it was a dive bar on the Upper East Side of Manhattan called American Trash. It was a notorious biker bar where I spent, or as my mom would say, wasted, several years of my early and mid-twenties.

At my mother's urging, ("you are never going to meet a nice man in that place"), I stopped going for two years, that is, until the night I met Jim. I was dating a man named Paul, who was a self-centered jerk. He was an only child who was spoiled rotten and had a sense of entitlement. One sultry summer evening, we had a huge fight during dinner at a midtown restaurant. I didn't feel like going home since it was early, so I stalked off in my red and white polka-dotted sundress (which is still hanging in my closet to this day) and walked over to my old home away from home, American Trash. When I walked in the door and assumed my favorite corner seat next to a window, I felt like Norm at Cheers.

While I sat in the corner, drinking an icy cold Budweiser Lite straight out of the bottle, I happened to eavesdrop on two young men having a conversation. They were sitting at the bar, discussing their work life and their non-existent social life. They were both in suits, which was intriguing as this establishment didn't get many suit types.

As I sat observing and eavesdropping, I noticed one in particular was a nice looking man albeit a bit overweight; however, he had a very handsome face and killer smile. I sat there, glued to my seat, peeling my beer label off like I always did, listening intently. After about a half hour had passed, the other man walked over to me, quite unexpectedly, and said, "Hi, why don't you join us? You're sitting there listening to our conversation so you might as well join us." I was mortified and felt the blood rush to my cheeks. Damn, totally busted. So I had a choice: I could politely say, "No thank you, I am good right here" or I could get up and join them mid-bar; I chose the latter.

When I made my way over, I was introduced to the guy who'd caught me eavesdropping; his name was Bill. After a moment, I was introduced to the cuter of the two who told me his name was Jim. We rhymed, Jim and Kim.

I must say, in the beginning he reminded me of Clark Kent. He was in a suit, was well-spoken and mild-mannered. However, as the night wore on and I saw the bartender yank on Jim's tie so he would throw his head back to do a shot, or several, of Jägermeister, I thought, "Wow, maybe you can't judge a book by its cover". So, in a semi-seedy biker bar in New York City called American Trash, I met my husband.

Jim loved to party but, then again, so did I. We were young, had no kids, worked hard and we also liked to play hard. We were what were called DINKS in the 90s: dual income, no kids. On the weekends we would kick back after our work week and have a couple of drinks. Jim was primarily a beer drinker but, if we went out, would order a gin and tonic before switching to his beloved beer. My drink of choice was Johnnie Walker Black or Stoli Crystal both just on the rocks – no mixers, hard core.

Once we started our family, the drinking and partying, at least for me, became more and more infrequent. I would occasionally have a glass of wine, but only on the weekends unless we were out, which was rare once our daughters were born. Shortly after we moved to Westchester, in 1995, he joined the Lions Club at his best friend and neighbor's urging. The Lions met every Tuesday and he loved it. He loved it so much that not only did he become the youngest Lion President in our town's history, I had "Dedicated Lion" inscribed on his headstone.

While they did and still do an incredible amount of charitable work for our community and various organizations, it is also extremely social. After the meetings, or even before, they would drink. So, every Tuesday night he began drinking. They also participated in a great deal of activities over the weekend so, again, more nights of drinking.

My big drinking days were few and far between at this point. Jim, however, was drinking more and more. I am not saying he was an alcoholic but, towards the end of his life, he started drinking heavily and seemed to be following in his father's footsteps. After all, alcoholism has a hereditary element. The worst part was that I had no idea how much he was drinking or the lengths to which he was going to hide it from me, until the end.

About ten days before he took his life, I heard strange noises coming from the basement. I went down to investigate. There he was, sitting at his desk with headphones on sobbing. I asked him what was wrong and at that moment he confessed that he had started drinking pretty much on a daily basis, sometimes even in the morning. How on earth was that possible? How was he functioning and functioning incredibly well at work? How did I not know? He said he was depressed and scared and I asked him, point blank, if he wanted to get in the car and I would take him to our local psychiatric hospital.

He immediately said, "What would I tell my boss?"

I said, "That you need some time off to be with your mom." His mom was diagnosed with breast cancer several months prior.

Then he said, "What would I tell our girls and my mother?"

I replied, "That you need to go on back to back business trips and wouldn't be home for a couple of weeks. Also, say that the cell service where you are going will be limited, so you might be out of touch for a few days."

Sadly, he made the decision not to go and I couldn't force him. He went to bed and while he was sleeping I went on the internet and wrote down every Alcoholics Anonymous meeting date and time starting down county in White Plains and all the way up the Hudson line. When he woke up and saw the list on his desk, he thanked me and seemed calmer and more relaxed, perhaps because his drinking secret was out.

Several days later, he went on a business trip as if nothing happened. When he returned home, I was at our neighbors', celebrating their daughter Kathy's birthday. I went outside to smoke a cigarette and saw his car in our driveway. I called and asked what time he got home and he told me an hour ago.

So I asked, "Why didn't you come over?" To which he replied, "I was afraid to as I don't want to be there if it's a big drinking scene." He thought that he wouldn't be able to socialize, especially with his buddy next door, if he wasn't drinking. He eventually came over, had one or two beers and came home. Several days later, he took his life. Many months after he died, I found empty vodka and beer bottles hidden all over his workshop and our garage.

Alcohol is a depressant and a very powerful one. I knew my husband was depressed, especially after his father died, but I had no idea to what extent. Several people I know whose spouses committed suicide said their spouses were drinking heavily before they ended their lives. Take it from me, alcohol and depression are a deadly combination.

Several years after Jim died, I went to my first Al-Anon meeting and, five years later, I am proud to say I still go when I can. Al-Anon is for people whose lives have become affected by someone else's drinking. It is an incredible program, which I happened to find very helpful and incredibly spiritual.

People have seen a change in me since I started attending meetings. When I attended my first meeting, I said it wasn't for me; I wouldn't be back. Well, the members encourage you to try six meetings before deciding, so I went back and kept going back and I am so glad I did. I am much calmer and do more things for myself, which I always thought was selfish. However, thankfully, through the grace of the program it has helped me change some of my negative thoughts and has certainly helped me emotionally. It also helps you understand the disease and the three C's: you didn't cause it, you can't control it and you can't cure it!

I wish I had known about Al-Anon when Jim was alive because I think it would have helped him understand who his father really was and how his father's drinking affected him. If your spouse or someone you know committed suicide, died from an alcohol-related disease, or was even killed by a drunk driver, I highly suggest you look into Al-Anon. Again, while it might not work for you, I encourage you to try it as it's just another tool to help you through the grieving process.

SUICIDE, THE HARDEST DEATH

To me, suicide is, by far, the hardest death to grieve. I am not trying to minimize the way your spouse or loved one died. From my point of view, suicide is harder for several reasons, which I will explain.

First, if you personally find that person, you are scarred for life. I will never, ever be the same. I saw something that sunny spring day that no one should ever have to witness. If you found your spouse or loved one, I am sure you would agree. Obviously, some suicides are more gruesome than others. As I mentioned, Jim's death was beyond horrific as he used a shotgun. He put the barrel of the gun in his mouth and somehow managed to pull the trigger. I was told, many years later, that he probably used a stick or a tool in his workshop to aid him. I hope to God I never see anything that disturbing or graphic in my life again. No one should have to see a loved one, mutilated and bloody with half a head, or with their face blue from being hanged.

Anytime someone mentions the word brains, ten years later my mind immediately goes to seeing his on the floor of his workshop.

It took years of therapy, and the help of my dear friend Valerie, to try and erase that image from my mind. Notice how I said try, as it will never truly be gone. When my mind wants to go to a dark place, that is exactly where it goes. If your spouse or anyone you know committed suicide, and used a gun in particular, you know it wasn't a cry for help; they wanted the job done and done right, the first and only time. When the Death Certificate reads, "Gunshot wound to the mouth and brain," you know that person meant business. Statistically, six out of ten suicide deaths are by the use of firearms.

I can finally admit that it enraged me that he took his life in this manner, and especially in our home. Thankfully, he did it in his workshop as it was a place the girls and I didn't go into often. If he had done it in our bedroom or God forbid, the kitchen, I would have never been able to stay in our home. If he wanted to take his life, why didn't he just drive off a cliff on his way home from that last business trip? My daughters and I would have thought he died in an accident. It would have been easier, emotionally, for all of us to handle.

Another thing that bothers me is, depending upon the manner in which they died, an open casket is out of the question. For me, that wasn't a big deal as I don't believe in open caskets; I personally think they are disturbing and unnecessary. For some people however, like my mother-in-law, my family and other relatives, I think that hurt them deeply. I truly believe people don't get closure with a closed casket.

Third, it leaves so many unanswered questions, especially like in the case of my late husband, because there wasn't a note. In one respect, I desperately wanted one. I wanted his final words, in writing, to me and our girls not only saying goodbye, but telling us what he was feeling and why, why he felt the need to end his life and destroy ours. Again, no closure. However, on the other hand, I was thankful there wasn't one because, to me, that would have meant that he gave it a great deal of thought, enough thought that he wrote his thoughts down, on paper, to be read not only by us, his family, but the police, strangers. I read that most, if not all suicide survivors claim they do not recall their actions leading up to their attempt. I have heard and have even spoken to a couple of suicide survivors who describe the feeling of being in a black hole and not being able to escape. They have no recollection of the attempt. I truly believe if my late husband had survived, he would have told me the same thing.

I will forever think of reasons why he did it, why he took his life and left me behind to grieve this horrible, lonely death. I will always think of things I wish I had said or done; however, if I said or did those things, would he still be here? Would it had made a difference?

No closure. None. Don't get me wrong, I have a theory as to why he did it, and, while I will never know, my theory gives me comfort.

What is my theory? I believe he saw himself becoming his father, a verbally abusive alcoholic, and he didn't want that life for me and our girls. In the beginning I took it personally. How could I not? How could he do this to me, to our girls, to us, to our lives?

Was life, here, with me and our daughters so bad that the only alternative was to take your life? I certainly pray not. I thought we had a good marriage. We were a team, we were Jim and Kim. I felt betrayed. I always used to say that when our girls got older, my husband would take care of the math homework and I would handle English. He broke up the team. Who will help them with their math homework? It turns out they had to rely on themselves over the years, as I can barely do grade school math.

Then I started thinking about all the times we fought or I would nag. I particularly thought long and hard about our last fight. Maybe I was a terrible wife and he just didn't want to be around me anymore. Could I have possibly driven him to it? Frankly, the more guilt, the more grief.

When he passed away, we were still very much a couple. Don't get me wrong, our marriage wasn't perfect. We had our issues like everyone else; however, when he died, we weren't fighting, neither of us was cheating nor were we in the middle of a separation or divorce. These issues would obviously change the way you grieve.

When I finally made the journey down to Florida to see my mom after Jim's wake and funeral, I could tell she was holding something back so, one night when I was down visiting, I said, "I know you want to say something, so say it." At which point she blurted loudly, "He was a selfish, selfish man." I never thought, and still don't to this day, that what he did was selfish.

Anyone who knew my late husband could attest to that. Unfortunately, my mother wasn't the only person I know who thought that; I heard it on several occasions.

I will admit some days I still have a really hard time believing he had a mental illness, which is why suicide is such a stigma to this day. Yes, I said it, stigma. It is and, unfortunately, I think it will be for a long time.

Here is an example. When a local woman lost her husband to a heart attack, the community set up scholarship funds for her children, but not for my children. Why? I am sure it is because of the manner in which he died. Community leaders didn't know how to handle it, so it was basically swept under the rug. Here's the real kicker. Jim's best friend, Rich, hanged himself from a tree in his mother's backyard ten years before, almost to the day that my husband took his life.

Jim was beside himself. Once he digested the news we heard that dreaded morning at 6:00 a.m., March 2, 1996, he said, "How could he do this to his mom and to me? I don't understand." After Jim spoke at his funeral, he admitted to me that he would never be able to forgive Rich. Ironic.

A friend of mine whose wife committed suicide is having a hard time because he cheated on her several times throughout their marriage. He claims he wasn't a model husband, so he feels directly responsible for her death. In addition, he is an ex-cop, a big burly man. He feels it was his job, not only as an ex-cop but as a man, a husband, to aid and comfort people in their time of need. He dropped his guard and someone he knew, his wife Debi, died on his watch. I keep telling him he has to stop feeling guilty; he didn't pull the trigger.

With a suicide, you also tend to put that person on a pedestal. You seem to remember only the good things he or she did, not the bad. Your brain reminds you of the good times you had, but not the horrible ones. Trust me, my late husband wasn't a saint but then again neither was I.

Friends never use the phrase "just shoot me" or "I want to blow my brains out" in front of me and if they do, unconsciously, they immediately apologize. It's just a saying. I say it myself.

Additionally, I don't know about you, but I have seen several friends who have died or are dying of a terminal illness, like cancer, and they did or are doing everything in their power to stay here in this life. So it is just incomprehensible when your loved one decides, with their healthy body, that they simple don't want to be here anymore.

Unimaginable.

I also know and have known friends with terminal illnesses who thought long and hard about taking their lives. I can understand that now, especially if the pain, whether emotional or physical, is too much to bear. If you are a widow/widower due to the suicide of your spouse, and your child is incredibly upset and has been acting out, your mind will now immediately think, "Will they take their life too?" Any other parent will just think it is normal teenage angst and it will pass. So unfair and, thankfully, mostly unfounded, but you worry nonetheless. Plus, mental illness is often hereditary, so your fear can be well-founded.

People also feel they have the right to weigh in on the issue of suicide, like they are experts. Some people are sympathetic, surmising that he/she must have been in a great deal of pain to do what they did. Others say, and I have heard it several times from several people, one being my mother, that their act was selfish.

My oldest daughter's religious instruction teacher told my daughter's class that anyone who commits suicide goes to Hell. I was furious when she told me several days after it happened. How dare she! The Catholic Church, which I have been a part of my whole life, now recognizes suicide as symptom of mental illness, which enables your loved one to now be buried in a Catholic cemetery.

As I am not an expert, I can only tell you what I know about my Jim. However, most people I have met over the years whose spouses committed suicide confirmed my thought as well. These people were clinically depressed and some, if not all, used alcohol to escape, which just exacerbates the depression. As we all know, alcohol is a depressant and a very powerful one.

Suicide, as you know, is related to mental illness which is hereditary. Jim's father got hit by a car one night because his children insisted he turn over his car keys for fear he would kill someone while drinking and driving. Instead, he got hit by a car walking home from a liquor store. He was on quite a tear prior to that night because he could not believe he'd outlived his second wife, who was eleven years his junior. She had died suddenly, at age 48, of a brain aneurism several months prior. He died four short months after her. He survived the accident; however, after it happened he clearly stated to my brother-in-law Brian, at the hospital, "I really did it this time." Unfortunately, his organs shut down because of the blunt force trauma and, the autopsy revealed, cirrhosis of the liver. Big surprise. Was it truly an accident or did he end his life? To this day, I will always wonder whether he purposely stepped in front of that car. Jim was never the same after that night.

I think it's important to mention a few statistics regarding suicides. First, it is the twelfth leading cause of death in the United States. Gun suicides have been on the rise in the past several years as more and more people are buying guns. Men are more likely to commit suicide by firearm. Tough economic conditions, unemployment, combat or simply being in the military contribute greatly to the suicide rate. The victims' ages vary year to year; however, people sixty-five and over, and males between the ages of forty-five and fifty-four tend to have the highest rates. These are just a few basic statistics.

There are so many studies being conducted. Believe it or not, there have been studies done that show a correlation of altitude above sea level wherein lack of oxygen might lead to depression. The bottom line is depression is usually at the root of suicide.

Unfortunately, I bet you know at least one person who has committed suicide; I know eight. That is a significant number. Deaths of this sort are usually hushed up and no one talks about them. Jim's brother didn't tell people how Jim had died for a long time because he said he wanted people to remember his brother for who he was, not how he died. I can understand that because the man who took his own life clearly wasn't the same person we had known in life. Once you start speaking about it, telling how your loved one died, someone will eventually mention that they had an aunt, a cousin, a friend, who died by their own hand. A sad but true fact.

Three years after Jim died, I finally summoned the courage to call the detective that was assigned to his case. After explaining who I was and the circumstances of his death, he said he remembered me. I told him that I wanted to know the results of the toxicology report. He seemed surprised but promised to pull Jim's file and would get back to me as soon as possible.

Well, the very next day the detective called and I was shocked and saddened all over again. Jim did not have any drugs or even alcohol in his system. I was, obviously, hoping that he drank that morning or took some pills or something, anything which would have made him literally out of his mind to do what he did. Unfortunately, that was not case and the mere surprise about that fact sent me into a downward spiral of depression for several weeks. My friend's wife died the same way and he told me he was praying the toxicology report would say she had a brain tumor.

A horrible thought but, sadly, it would have made things better.

I have said this line many times after Jim took his life, and after I heard that my favorite comedian, Robin Williams, had committed suicide, I said it again. Their pain and suffering is over; it's the ones they leave behind whose pain and suffering has just begun.

I still have days, ten years later, where I get incredibly mad thinking that he made a conscience choice to leave our daughters and me. I know it's not rational, nor was he being rational at the time. There are so many unanswered questions and there always will be, which is why, to me, suicide is the hardest death.

TIME FOR SOME CHANGES

No matter when your loved one passed away, whether it was a month, a year, or several years ago, the best thing you can do is work on change. I am sure you are thinking, "change what?" Well, there really are lots of things you can change, but here are some things I found helpful.

First, I changed my bedroom. I started by totally rearranging the furniture. I found this extremely difficult to do emotionally, because we'd had our bedroom the same way since the day we bought our home. However, because he was no longer there on his side of the bed when I looked over in the middle of the night, it was unbearable. It was impossible to get a good night's sleep. So, one day I decided to move every piece of furniture except for our armoire (only because it fit perfectly in its spot). It was strange the first day or so, but not only did I get used to it, I actually preferred it and wondered why we never thought to try it this way.

Next, I changed all the bedding, such as the sheets, comforter, and the bed's decorative pillows. I even bought new curtains. I actually hated to buy these as I am terrible at picking them out. My late husband selected every window treatment in our home. To pull the "look" all together, I added a small, white fluffy area rug. To complete the room, I bought several large glass urns to hold my seashell and sea glass collections which I have been hoarding since I was 18 years old.

Finally, I asked my talented bereavement buddy Candace, whom I had met in group, to paint all the walls. The room was eggshell colored, like most of our house, and I had her paint the walls two different colors, a sea green base, ragged over with metallic silver so that it would remind me of the deep sea. The bedroom became my room, not our room. While sad, it was necessary.

Second, I tackled Jim's clothes, which was a very difficult, but necessary job and didn't cost anything. When do you get rid of your spouse's clothes? Again, there is no right or wrong time, I have come to find out that everyone is different. Some people in my bereavement group got rid of everything almost immediately; the sight and the smell was too much to bear. Others took care of this issue a couple of years later. Some, many years later, still had every stitch. I was somewhere in the middle. I gave away lots of his suits to his brother and gave my brother other pieces. I gave out his fancy silk ties to various old friends. I also kept one for each of my daughters and I use his Lions tie to hold together my yoga mat. I donated the rest. However, I will admit that to this day, and I am not quite sure why, I still have some of his favorite shirts in a tiny corner of my closet.

Third, I decided to rip out the rug in our family room. I never really wanted a rug in that room because we had French doors leading out to our deck and I felt the outdoor foot traffic would destroy the rug in no time. However, since it was where my baby girls would spend most of their time and would learn to crawl, it had to be carpeted. But ten years and multiple stains later, it was time for it to come up and refinish the beautiful hardwood floors hiding beneath. Again, another wonderful decision.

My next project was to redo the bathroom in our bedroom; a costly but very necessary job. I always said the reason my husband and I stayed married was because we had separate bathrooms. His was a tiny bathroom with a stall shower in our bedroom and mine was down the hall. The girls were small at the time but I knew that in the blink of an eye, they would become teenagers. I do not think anyone in their right mind would want to share a bathroom with two teenagers, especially two teenage girls.

Now they are seventeen and fourteen and if you have teenagers, especially daughters, I am sure you agree. I can honestly tell you that was the best decision regarding the house that I have made to date.

The home renovations, however, devastated me, not only financially but emotionally.

My late husband was a master at building even though it wasn't his chosen profession. He could build anything and was that way even as a child; the only good thing he learned from his father.

People and even professionals were amazed at his workmanship.

Over the years, he built our deck, porch, gutted and redid two bathrooms, designed and built our basement playroom and bar, created a new mantelpiece, put up crown molding in our living room, and even built permanent shelves in our family and bedrooms. I had no idea how much money he saved us over the years doing these projects himself until I started getting quotes to redo the little bathroom in our bedroom. The contractors wanted huge amounts of money! So every time I did a renovation, it devastated me in more ways than one. If you are a widow and you had to hire someone to do something that your husband normally would have fixed, you understand exactly what I am talking about.

In addition to home renovations, I changed other things as well. The first year Jim died, I asked my girls where they wanted to put our Christmas tree. We used to have it in our living room in front of the picture window. It is a nice place for a tree because it is a bigger room and has a fireplace. However, the girls decided they did not want it there after Jim died; they wanted to put it in our family room. I agreed since we spend more time in that room. Because it has a beamed ceiling, another project my late husband did in our home, we were able to get a bigger tree which we have been enjoying year after year.

Also, we used to drive to my husband's mother's house on Christmas Day. The first year he died, much to my mother-in-law's chagrin, I made the decision to go to our neighbor's house. Not having to rip my daughters away from their new toys on Christmas morning to head to Long Island with all the other holiday travelers was a huge relief. It was so nice to wander across the lawn midday to be with friends.

Finally, his death also changed something in me; it changed the way I looked at life and death. Ever since I was a kid, I had been afraid of death. I would go out to dinner with my dad and he would talk about what he thought the afterlife or Heaven was like. He would say how wonderful he thought it would be seeing his parents and other deceased friends and relatives. He said it would be like a big party, a celebration.

While this doesn't sound frightening, it was upsetting to hear as a child. When you are a child, you think everyone lives forever, especially your parents. To hear him talk about his own mortality was terrifying and it saddened me so much that every time he mentioned death, I would start crying hysterically no matter where I was. Sissy-pot, as my mom used to call me.

With the passing of my husband and both my parents, and my religious connection stronger since both, I can honestly say I no longer fear death. I used to have to take a Xanax to go to a wake or funeral, but not anymore. I am no longer afraid to die. When it is my time, it is my time. This is exactly what my dad used to say.

Next, it changed how I looked at life. I used to live in the past or in the future, now I live in the present as you never know what tomorrow will bring. I try to live each day to the fullest and without regrets. I say "I love you" daily and "I am sorry" often. I am grateful for everything I have and thank God every day. I get together with various friends throughout my life and go out for drinks or dinner. I am always throwing parties, barbecues or brunches so I can see my family, cousins and friends all of whom I adore. I use my good china now, my beautiful crystal and wear my good perfume even to go grocery shopping.

So, you see, not all change is bad.

GROUNDED – YOGA AND OTHER HEALING TECHNIQUES

When Jim died, I was in my fifth year of practicing yoga. I had always wanted to try it so I went to a class that was offered at a local school and instantly fell in love with the art and my wonderful instructor. If you have never taken a yoga class, I recommend you consider one.

My yoga instructor, Rona, started holding classes out of her home after the trial period at the school ended; I became an instant follower. She was such an incredible help to me after my husband died. Everything she'd taught me, however, went out the window the day Jim took his life. I was totally uprooted. I could and would crumple to the floor without warning. I forgot the most important aspect of yoga: I forgot how to breathe.

The day of Jim's death, a crime scene clean-up crew came to our home to clean up the horrific mess left behind. The first night, they came and scraped his brains off the floor and mopped up all the blood. My brother and sister, to this day, say they will never forget the smell of the disinfectant.

The next day, the crew came back to chop up Jim's two large homemade work benches because they were blood-soaked. I thankfully remember Rona's words to me at this point. She said, "You have to stay grounded to this earth. In order to be grounded to this earth, you must be as close to the earth as possible." When she saw the blank look on my face indicating that I was totally confused, she further explained,

"Go outside, take off your shoes and socks and walk barefoot in the grass."

I remember the feeling to this day, the way the cool grass felt beneath my feet as I walked around my property. While I was doing this, Jim's workbench was being cut up and tossed out the basement window on to the lawn, right where I was walking. I barely acknowledged it and just kept walking. I must say, those were incredible words of wisdom which I will never forget.

After a long while, I truly did feel connected and rooted in the world, my world which had become so unstable and off balance since that life-changing afternoon.

After all the work the clean-up crew put in those two days, they never found the bullet that ended his life. It was probably lodged in the wood they had just broken up and thrown away.

For months, in the morning, I would do an asana, which means pose, called tree. Tree is a balancing pose. You rock back and forth putting all your weight in your feet until you feel rooted. Once you feel your feet are firmly planted in the ground, you put one foot on the inside thigh of the other leg. Once you feel you are solidly grounded, you put your arms together over your head. If you can hold tree for more than thirty seconds without toppling over, you are pretty well grounded. It was my test every morning for many months. I still do this, ten years later.

When your loved one dies, you essentially forget how to breathe. Truth be told, no one breathes properly. If you want to know how to breathe, watch a baby especially when they are sleeping. Their stomach goes up and down with every breath. We, as a society, are constantly trying to hold in our stomachs, which results in us taking shallow breaths. Breath work is so important. There are several yoga breaths; some calm you and others energize you. Take a deep breath in through your nose, hold it to the count of three then slowly release the air through your nose. That breath alone can calm you, relax you and, if you concentrate, you can actually visually breathe into a particular spot on your body and help it relax or even heal.

The night Jim died, and for several nights after, my dear friend Juliette would climb in bed with me and practice Reiki. Reiki is a Japanese technique for stress reduction and relaxation, and it also promotes healing. When a Reiki healer puts their hands on you, they can spiritually guide life force energy. When she worked on me, I felt exactly what they say about the art; I felt a glowing radiance through and around me and instantly felt calmer. I know it sounds crazy, but I feel you shouldn't judge it until you have tried it.

My yoga instructor was also a Reiki Master, which allows her to teach the art. She would often give classes on how to become a Reiki I healer but, unfortunately, I had my hands full with my girls and our new life and was never able to get to one of her classes.

In addition to being certified in Hatha and Kundalini yoga, Rona also knew various other forms such as Vinyasa and Yin, each very different and beneficial in their own ways. Besides teaching yoga and Reiki, she is also a shamanic healer. What is a shamanic healer? A Shaman, as they are called, helps specifically with healing the soul.

Soul loss, as it is called, is a survival mechanism that takes place during painful and traumatic events. When this occurs, part of our soul leaves during trauma in order for the psyche to survive the experience. Lord knows I had suffered a traumatic experience and had lost part of my soul, so you can imagine how overjoyed I was to learn this was one of her many talents. Her skills continued to heal me. A week or so after Jim died she came and smudged my house.

Smudging a house is a spiritual cleansing to clear one's body aura and home from negative energy. It is performed by lighting a piece of sage on fire and fanning the smoke over rooms in the home. I would think someone dying in your home, especially by their own hand, constitutes negative energy. To this day, I actually still practice this on occasion. If someone visits my home and is either sick or, more importantly, has an incredibly negative aura, I will sage my house after they leave.

Additionally, I don't usually use over-the-counter medicines to feel better when I am sick; I always try holistic medicine first. I have found they work incredibly well a great deal of the time, and they are all natural. I used chamomilla when my daughters were babies and teething. I drank loquat syrup when I had a croupy cough the day of Jim's funeral. I take my Echinacea blend when I get the first sign of feeling run down and have fought off countless colds. One daughter has tried holy basil leaf for stress. I have taken and still take pulsatilla and Kali Bi when the colds I have had warranted their use. Currently, I am trying black cohosh to combat my new menopausal symptoms.

I would much rather seem a little nutty and do yoga, chant, light a candle and meditate than take anti-depressants, which is what more than eighty percent of my bereavement group was taking; I was one of the few exceptions. I took Xanax for several weeks after Jim's death but it was more because of my PTSD. I stopped before I started therapy or my bereavement group, all on my own.

I truly believe that if I didn't have all the above-mentioned tools, I would have remained on Xanax and might have even moved on to the heavier meds my new bereavement friends were taking.

I know yoga, holistic medicine and many of these other practices may sound completely foreign to you, maybe even downright ridiculous; however, please remember that the above-mentioned practices and herbs have been in existence for thousands of years. You can read about each and every one of them, and hear about the many benefits; you don't have to take my word. I will, however, tell you that every time I do yoga, I sleep like a baby and say, "I should do this more often." Every time I do deep yoga breathing, I get my heart rate to go down dramatically. When I sage my house, there is a calmness within. Almost every time I take holistic herbs, I get better. I know these practices work. As I always say to those who ask me about these practices, "You have nothing to lose and everything to gain."

MY HIGHER POWER

I have said it on more than one occasion. If I did not have a higher power, whom I happen to call God, in my life when my husband took his, I personally do not think I would have survived.

Being raised in a Roman Catholic household, religion was a big part of my life growing up. Sunday mass was a must in my family. My mother would wear her Sunday best and drag me, my brother and two sisters to the 11:45 a.m. mass at St. Augustine's in New City, New York.

Certainly, as a child, mass was the last place you wanted to be on a Sunday morning. The only way you got out of going was to basically be on your deathbed. My dad, who was an usher and an early riser, preferred to go to the 7:30 a.m. mass.

I attended a Catholic school, St. Augustine's, from kindergarten to sixth grade. I was terrified of the nuns. When I started there, most still wore habits. They were incredibly strict and frightening, especially as a child, and they left quite an impression on me. While these nuns were scary, the nuns of my parents' generation were much worse. My father used to tell me stories about getting whacked on the knuckles on a regular basis with a ruler.

When my sister Laura and I got old enough to attend mass ourselves, we used to cut mass preferring to hang out in the back of the orange building (an office building on Main Street that is literally bright orange). However, before we returned home, we would have to sneak into the church and get a bulletin to bring home to our mom to prove we actually attended. After a few Sundays, she figured we weren't going to mass so she would proceed to grill us on the homily.

Once or twice we made something up, but again, my mom knew we weren't going.

Because I entered junior high, or middle school as it is now called, straight out of a Catholic school I was treated like a freak. Friendships had been established long ago so when I got there, I was basically an outcast and spent a great deal of time alone. It was as if I had moved there from another planet and I was threatened with a beating on a weekly basis. I barely survived those years and, thankfully, went on to have a wonderful time in high school.

When I turned 17, I graduated high school and went off to a business school in New Haven, Connecticut. While I was there, I never went to mass. I was out of my parent's house and it was my decision.

I moved to New York City when I turned 19. Again, I didn't join a parish or attend mass. I was on my own and it was my choice and I chose not to. I would much rather go to Sunday brunch, than listen to some boring priest yammer on. That year, my beloved dad died of a massive heart attack on his way home from the hospital. I became enraged at God. Following my dad's death, I would ask Him over and over again, "Why? He didn't deserve to die, especially so young, at 54. How could you let a good, hardworking, incredibly generous man die, leaving us behind, especially since there are such scums of the earth, murderers, rapists, child molesters still running around?" At that point, I turned my back on God and the church.

I didn't go back to church until I met my husband ten years later and was forced to go to Pre-Cana classes in preparation for our marriage. In addition to Pre-Cana classes, I had to go to confession, something I had not done in over fifteen years! My future husband and I attended an all-day Sunday Pre-Cana class, which was basically torture. The only thing I took with me and find true to this day is, we were told, "Never fight when you are tired and hungry." I have come to realize that is a true statement and works for anyone, not just your spouse. Confession after 15 years was interesting. I had lots to tell having not been there for so long. I confessed my sins, some mild, some not so mild, to a nice, patient priest who, thankfully, listened without asking any questions. He told me I was absolved and that God forgives me. When I emerged, I had to say a whole bunch of Hail Mary prayers.

When it was my fiancé's turn, he fared far worse. He got an old-fashioned priest who asked him many personal questions. Once he found out my husband-to-be and I were living together (in sin), he raked him over the coals. Jim emerged sweating profusely, and swore he would never go back to confession again and I believe he never did.

Once we were married, I slacked off. I would go to mass sporadically but made consistent trips to church on the holidays. I prayed when I was worried or wanted something; however, it wasn't part of my daily life. All this changed when I became a mother. Once I held my first baby girl in my arms, I knew she was truly a gift and a blessing from God. I experienced a fierce need to protect her and felt I needed God's help to watch over her. A month later, we met with our priest and a lovely nun at our parish to get information regarding our baby girl's baptism. The ceremony was on a lovely spring day in May and from that moment on, I went to mass every Sunday. Not because I had to but because I wanted to; that was the difference.

Since my parish did so much for me during and after Jim's death, I, in turn, wanted to do something nice for them so I joined two other women from my parish, Dede and Linda and started cleaning our little one-hundred-plus-year-old church every Thursday. My girlfriend, Bobbi (Barbara) calls us "The God Squad."

All I can tell you is that being there stilled my mind. I enjoyed the quiet. I prayed the whole time I cleaned, which left me feeling unburdened. I put family and friends' names in the prayer book when they needed help. I believe in the power of prayer. It has been ten years since my late husband's death. While our hundred-plus-year old, sweet country church no longer exists, I now help clean our brand-new ultra-modern church still every Thursday.

My faith was tested yet again when my mom died very quickly fourteen short months after my late husband. She was diagnosed with three cancers and was at stage four when detected. I know this is going to sound crazy but I sincerely think Jim died in order to prepare me for my mother's death. My mom and I were incredibly close and I don't think I would have been able to handle her death without fully experiencing Jim's prior demise.

Additionally, it was my mother's deep faith that got me through her death as she accepted that she was dying and that The Lord and my dad in Heaven were waiting for her. If she accepted that she was dying, and had an unwavering faith while looking death straight in the eye, why shouldn't I?

While I believe in God, Judgment Day, Heaven and other aspects of my religion, it is far from perfect. I must say I am glad the Catholic Church at least now recognizes suicide as a mental illness and allows you to be buried in a Catholic cemetery, not that Jim is, nor would he care.

There is so much about the Catholic Church and its teachings that I simply don't agree with; however, I won't bore you with my beliefs. Let's just say, I take out of my religion what I need and want and leave the rest.

I felt so lost and alone after Jim died. I didn't know where to turn. I personally turned to God because I felt I HAD to or I wouldn't have survived the ordeal. I had to turn it over to Him or it would have overwhelmed me to the point where I wouldn't have been able to function.

My daughters and I say grace every night and often say what we are thankful for. They regularly attend mass with me, but I know they won't much longer and that's okay because I take comfort knowing that someday they will come back to their faith when they need and want to.

I have two friends who have lost their spouses. One grew up with no religion in her life and she is desperately trying to find a faith for her young son who is craving religious structure.

The other grew up in a very strict Catholic home, but gave up on his religion long ago and now is very angry and feels God betrayed him. Needless to say, he is stuck in his grieving process.

Here is something else. If you have faith and believe your loved ones can see and hear you, I am here to tell you I truly believe they can and do. When my dad died, my family and I kept finding pennies. Pennies from Heaven. When my mom died, we decided to make her a dime as she would have to trump my dad. I cannot tell you how many times my brother, sisters and I found dimes after she died. Now, we always seem to find dimes and pennies together. In the wash, on the street, or as change after a purchase. I recently found a dime, a penny and a nickel (which represents Jim) at the hospital when my youngest daughter had surgery. I know it sounds unbelievable, but I swear it is true. Additionally, Jim loved the rock band Pink Floyd so much so that I actually put the words, "Shine On" on his headstone which is part of the name of one of their songs.

After he died, I would hear Pink Floyd songs so much that it was getting eerie. My mom did not me believe me at first until we got in the car one day to go to my daughter Samantha's dance recital and the Pink Floyd song, "Wish You Were Here" came on and my oldest, Alexandra, said, "I guess Daddy's coming to the recital." Through the years he has "shown up" through Pink Floyd songs so much that I coined the phrase, "We are being Floyded." I don't think there has been one major event in either of our daughters' lives that he hasn't appeared through song.

Several of my bereavement friends have said similar things have happened to them too. Coincidence? I truly don't think so. I have been told by my writing group friend Mary that when you start receiving signs, your loved one has arrived. When signs of your loved one start to slow down or stop all together it means your grief is winding down and you are ready to move forward.

Since I have met Bryon, I barely get "Floyded" anymore. Looking back, I am glad my parents made me go to church and that I had a religion to fall back on when I needed it the most.

I was rooted in faith, which helped me survive their deaths. It gave me comfort and peace, which I desperately needed. I am not saying that you need to run off to your place of worship, just know that it is there if you need it. If you weren't raised with a particular faith, there are plenty out there to try if you are so inclined. I encourage you to try several until you find one that suits you best.

THE OUTLAWS

The definition of outlaw is a lawless person or habitual criminal. These definitions do not apply to my in-laws so why do I use that word to describe my late husband's family? I never used to call them the outlaws; I started to when Jim died.

When you marry, not only do you marry that person but you marry their family and even their friends, for better or worse – as in-laws or outlaws.

First of all, I am not the only person I know who uses that term, far from it; however, most people who use the phrase outlaw to describe their in-laws use it in a negative sense. They are the bad guys. However, to clarify, when I use the term it is different. It just means they are out—not in—which isn't necessarily bad, just accurate. It is the reason I started calling them that since Jim died. It made more sense.

I was fortunate to marry into a good family; however, Jim's parents were divorced so, unfortunately, I married into not one but two families. While one was nice and normal, the other was strange and extremely dysfunctional. His father and his second wife, Linda, were the dysfunctional ones but since they both pre-deceased Jim, all ties were severed a few years prior to his death.

I had a nice mother-in-law or should I say have? Another dilemma. She's technically not my mother-in-law anymore. I never called her Mom because, to me, I had only one mom and she earned and deserved that title and I was not about to give it to anyone else. I introduce her as my late husband's mother, and I just call her what I have always called her, by her name, Marianne.

In the beginning weeks after Jim died, I kept in touch with Marianne and Jim's sister, Lynda, quite frequently. However, after several months had passed if one of us was sad and thinking of Jim, we wouldn't call each other for fear of triggering the other person. If I was having a decent day emotionally, and one of them called me crying, I would end up being sad and upset as well. I just couldn't help it.

I can only speak from experience, but when I was sad and would call one of them, I did it because I wanted to talk to someone who really knew him, as I was so baffled by the way he died. I was not in the mode where misery loves company. Not at all.

As the months passed, the calls started getting more and more infrequent. Let's face it, I was a reminder that he was no longer living. If they didn't talk to me, it was easier; they could almost pretend, at least for a little while, that it hadn't happened. I totally get it. I, on the other hand, didn't have a choice as I was living and breathing the tragedy on a daily basis. They didn't find his body. They weren't in the home where he lived and died. I didn't blame them in the least.

Marianne didn't visit often in the months after Jim died, but I understood; it was too hard to visit the home of her deceased son. It wasn't just difficult for Marianne. Everyone we knew felt that way, especially when it came to going downstairs to our bar, as Jim's workshop was right there, next door. For this reason, no one could understand how I could stay in the house and, while it was difficult, it was a choice and I chose to stay for the stability of our daughters.

Their world was already in upheaval; I didn't want to add to it by ripping them away from their home.

We all know someone, I'm sure, who has horror stories about their in-laws, especially their monster-in-law. When I used to go to my bereavement group, I heard so many stories about people severing ties with their outlaws, all for various reasons. The family of one of my friends in my group tried to get their hands on their son's insurance money, attempting to leave her and her baby virtually penniless. Another's outlaws, couldn't stand to see her as it was too painful a reminder of their now deceased son. A friend, whose husband committed suicide, was practically blamed by her mother-in-law for his death and wanted nothing to do with her and her children. Sad.

Not all outlaws are bad; I also heard some really great stories about how loving and incredibly helpful they were months, even years after their child's death.

When I used to tell Marianne these stories, she was mortified. She assured me that would never happen with us. She would have to do or say something pretty awful for that to happen.

While she came very close one day when she said something horrific about my deceased mother, I became the better person and rose above her incredibly hurtful comments. And that's because I wouldn't want to hurt my outlaw by taking away her granddaughters. Hadn't she suffered enough? Hadn't my girls? I certainly wouldn't want them to experience another loss.

Let's face it, my girls are the last living link to my late husband, her son. If you look at my oldest daughter, Alexandra, she is the image of Jim.

Now, ten years later, Marianne comes to visit on special occasions or around the holidays to see my girls and go to the cemetery. A couple of years after Jim died and I started dating, she would come up and babysit, which was very gracious. That couldn't have been easy for her, seeing me move on.

Since my mom passed away fourteen months after Jim, Marianne became my daughter's only grandparent.

Now that my daughters are older, just turned seventeen and fourteen, she doesn't babysit anymore. She does come to Alexandra's drama class plays and chorus concerts and Samantha's cheerleading competitions, which is very sweet and my girls appreciate her being there showing her love and support.

I hope, at least for your children's sake, if you have children, that you make an effort to maintain a relationship with the outlaws. Sometimes it can be an effort, but in the end, it's worth it. Be the better person. Swallow your pride if you have to. It is important that your children have a connection to their grandparents, aunts and uncles as they are the ones who know all the stories - stories you yourself don't even know about your husband or wife. I urge you to think long and hard before you come to a final decision.

WILLS AND WHATNOT

It's amazing to me how many people I know, my sisters Laura and Karen included, that do not have a Will. If you didn't have one when your spouse died, I cannot imagine what you went through. Jim had a Will but the whole process was still a nightmare.

I personally think a great deal of people don't have Wills because the hardest part is not deciding who is going to be your executor, or who is going to get your favorite ring. It often comes down to who is going to be your children's guardian. Not only is death an uncomfortable subject, your own death, your own mortality is put in the forefront of your existence.

No matter what your beliefs, we all have to die sometime, so wouldn't you rather be prepared and know that your loved ones, especially your children, if you have them, will be taken care of by a responsible person?

Inheritance is only one part of the subject. More importantly, children need to be placed with someone you have deemed suitable. This person or people should be someone your children want to be with and are close enough to you to know all your old stories. That, to me, is one of the most important aspects of finding an appropriate guardian. Memories, telling the stories that will keep you alive in their minds.

My husband and I completed our Wills after our daughters were born. And, yes; the hardest part was deciding who was going to be their guardian. I was very grateful we made the decision and had it in place when my husband took his life barely four years later. Even though we had a Will, the probate process was still a difficult and daunting procedure. It's also expensive as you have to pay a lawyer to handle it and their fees are on an hourly basis. If you don't have a Will, I would advise you to have one drawn up as soon as possible.

Jim was very meticulous with certain things and, thankfully, one of those things was his filing system. In his desk in our basement, he kept all our household bills and policies. When he died, anyone could easily find what they were looking for; one being his Will. I suggest if you have a Will, you keep it in a safe place, but also a well-known spot for your executor to locate.

Having an efficient filing system is also really important and a gift to the executor; it makes an unbearable task simple and logical.

Okay, so we had Wills when Jim took his life and while it was obvious that the children and all his possessions would come to me upon his death, I knew at that moment I would have to do my own Will over. It wasn't just because Jim wasn't going to be their guardian when I died, but because there were other people we put in our Wills that I knew wouldn't be a big part of *my* life anymore. Clearly, some adjustments needed to be made.

To draw up Wills isn't as expensive as you might think, so if that's a reason you've put off, now is the time to do a little research and find a local attorney. Believe it or not, there are also simple Wills on the Internet that can be downloaded for a nominal fee.

Making a Will is extremely important. Think about the people in your life and what role you would like them to play. Who would be your best choice for guardian? Do they share your philosophy on parenting? Do they know your children well? Do they want to be the guardians?

Religion is another consideration. Next, think about picking someone to be your executor and keep him or her separate from the guardian. You can even indicate that you want a certain financial institution to oversee your children's inheritance or a trusted friend who is savvy with money.

Keeping the financial institution and the guardian separate helps keep the guardian accountable and honest when it comes to spending your children's inheritance.

If your children are young, you should consider a trust so that your children won't collect the bulk of your estate until they reach a certain age. Frankly, I think 21 is too young and opted for 25 so that, hopefully, my daughters will be more settled and grounded.

I also suggest that you write a letter to each of your children, in your handwriting, telling them about the day they were born. This is one of the best gifts you can give them. Our first parish priest asked us to write a letter to each of our daughters when they were born, which were to be given to them when they turned 13. Unfortunately, Jim never wrote his letter to Samantha, which was heartbreaking. I have other letters written to each of my girls that I add to and try and update every few years. I think it's important that they open one on each milestone birthday, just in case you're not there to celebrate with them. It's an upsetting yet comforting thought, at least to me.

In addition to a Will and a Living Will, I have specific instructions of how I want to be interred. I think it's important that the details be written down, especially whether you want to be buried or cremated, if you want a funeral or just a memorial service, or you have a notion of having no ceremony at all.

Being a widow or widower, you no longer have a spouse who knows your wishes. Does your family know what you have in mind? Your executor? They probably know some of the details, but not all. It's best to have it in writing. Again, another thing to be sure of that will give you peace of mind.

Here is another thing I am in the process of doing. I think you should write down a list of people you would like notified of your passing. When my late husband died, my friend Juliette took my phone book and started notifying people. Once my immediate family and Jim's family were called, they were the ones who thought of who needed to be called next.

Of course, the inevitable happened; several people weren't notified. Unfortunately, it happens all the time. Most times it's an oversight, but time and time again, people take it personally and actually get infuriated that they weren't informed.

Since phone books are basically a thing of the past, all your friends, family and acquaintances are stored in your phone. I suggest writing a list and periodically updating it and attaching it to your Will. Or putting an asterisk near the names of the people in your contact list you would like to be notified. Obviously, someone close to you needs to have the code to your phone for access to said list.

If family members are using your cell phone, I recommend using an asterisk because everyone has an eclectic group of contacts listed in their phones. While I think you would want your aunt or high school friend to know of your passing, you might not necessarily think your tailor or dog groomer needs to be notified.

When my daughters were born, my mom put aside pieces of jewelry and placed them in boxes with a little handwritten note. She instructed me to have them open the boxes on their sixteenth birthdays. She wanted me to have them just in case she wasn't there and it turns out, she wasn't. When I gave Alexandra her box, she read my mom's note and burst into tears. It was truly a gift from beyond; it was genius that my mother had enough foresight to make this incredible gesture. Even though my daughter got a used car for her birthday, I think she treasured her grandmother's gift even more because it was so special. I hope I get to do the same for my grandchildren someday.

Now, you have a Will in place and you think you're done. Think again. Life and circumstances change all the time and, with that, so must your Will. Originally, my sister, Laura, was to be my daughters' guardian, it made perfect sense. No one knows you like your own sister and besides, we were extremely close growing up and still are to this and married and her children lived with her. Now, she is divorced and her two sons, Paul and Luke are out of the house, Luke is in his last year of college, and Paul lives and works in New York City. Her daughter, Melissa, whom my daughters adore, just left for college this fall. Now, it's not so perfect.

The problem now is that my girls don't want to live with my sister and her "on again, off again" boyfriend, Danny, and his young son, Dylan. They also don't want to live in New Jersey. Now what? My daughters are in their mid-teens and have a say in where and with whom they would like to be placed, that is, until they turn 18. So, yes, I am in the process of redoing my Will yet again.

Recently, I have had several health scares. Thankfully, these issues forced me and my daughters to sit down and discuss their guardianship. After many conversations, they decided that they wanted my sister Laura to be their guardian but they wanted her to move into our home until they finished High School.

I, of course, then had to speak to my sister Laura and she agreed. If they didn't choose, I inevitably was going to have to choose for them; however, they would have still been able to petition the court for Right of Refusal. Additionally, should something happen to my sister, who has her own health issues, I have a back-up guardian in place. It's called "being prepared".

Since my recent medical problems, my daughters and I have also sat down and discussed certain pieces of my jewelry that they would like to eventually own. I must say, I am glad I was able to sit with them and go through the big items and hear what they would like and why. Maybe next time we sit down we will discuss paintings and other possessions.

Having a Will in place will give you and your children peace of mind (see Down One Parent chapter) especially if you have unresolved or continuing health issues.

So, my advice to you is if you don't have a Will yet, start combing through your family, relatives and even close friends to select an appropriate guardian, executor, and a financial expert to oversee the finances. Once you decide who's right for you and your family, you need to talk to them. Remember, there is the possibility that they will say no, so make sure you have more than one choice picked out, just in case.

THE WIDOW'S/WIDOWER'S CARD

My late friend, Adam, jokingly used to say he and his friends had man cards and when any of them did or said anything remotely feminine, or acted like a wuss, they would say to each other, "Turn in your man card".

Well, believe it or not, widows and widowers have widow's/widower's cards; however, our cards are a bit different. They can be used in various ways, for solely your benefit and, unfortunately, cannot be revoked.

If you are newly widowed, you might not be familiar with this term. At first, you might be disturbed by it because you don't want to play the victim; however, you will not only use it but, at times, you will embrace it. I know it's probably not right to do, almost like some kind of bizarre entitlement, but especially in the early stages of grief it can be incredibly helpful and, believe me, you are going to need all the help you can get to survive, especially the first year.

Let me give you a few examples:

In the beginning, you will be consumed with endless amounts of paperwork and some things are bound to slip between the cracks. If you're late with a bill, mortgage payment, or a renewal, you can use the widow's/widower's card and explain how you lost your spouse and they used to take care of such things. You will get an obligatory "I'm sorry for your loss" usually followed by, "No problem, just get the payment to us as soon as you can". I used it a great deal in the beginning especially for that reason. Jim took care of the bills and I was so overwhelmed with the finances and the day-to-day running of the house, as well as our daughters, that I found it impossible to keep up with everything, especially the household bills.

I have pulled my "W/W" card out to get a doctor appointment for either myself or my girls.

Keeping us well, especially myself as I was a one-woman show, and being healthy was my main priority. I remember one specific time when I used it with one of Samantha's doctor to give us her special back brace for her scoliosis at cost, since my lousy, low-income insurance wouldn't cover it. They don't cover what's called "durable medical equipment," which is ridiculous. So, instead of paying $2,300 for her body brace, I paid $1,000. While still a crazy amount of money, it was certainly better and, believe me, every little bit helps.

I've used it to get upgrades when we travelled, whether it was better plane seats, upgraded rental car or hotel. This was incredibly helpful as I was now traveling alone with young children. I was given free summer camp for my girls. I rarely used it, as they both were absolutely miserable there, but it was nice to have when I needed it.

All the stress from my new life and grief had me clenching my teeth so hard during the night that I would wake up with a sore jaw. After a couple of weeks of pain, I made an appointment to see my dentist. He looked in my mouth and noticed that I had been doing an incredible amount of grinding. The only way to stop me from wearing down my teeth to nubs was to make me a special guard for my mouth. Once he learned of Jim's death, he refused to let me pay for it. A gesture to this day I will never forget.

One year, my church's senior group made me and my girls hand-knitted scarves and mittens. They also bought us each a small gift. So thoughtful and sweet. No widow's/widower's card needed!

The last act of kindness was by my church's Monsignor. He was one of the priests that presided over Jim's funeral. Not only did he not let me pay for their religious instruction that year, he had flowers delivered to my home every Easter, Thanksgiving, and Christmas up until the time he retired, last year. Additionally, every Christmas he gave me an envelope at mass and told me to buy my girls each something that they didn't get for Christmas. He was the sweetest man I have ever known and I miss him terribly.

Unfortunately, not all people are as generous so the card has its uses. It's great to use if you have to leave work early or avoid a frivolous function. Remember, you're alone now so if your child is sick or needs to be somewhere, you have no choice but to use one to get out of work or the function altogether.

I will admit there were times when I used it shamelessly. Once, I used my card to get my children a private sliming at a kid hotel (if you have a child, you will know what that means).

Additionally, when I felt my girls needed more attention at school, I would use it on their teachers; however, only in the beginning.

So, how long can you use your widow's/widower's card? You can almost use it indefinitely, or at the very least until you remarry. I used it for many years. Truth be told, I still use it occasionally to this day, ten years later, if the situation warrants its use. Remember, however, that you risk someone asking you how long your spouse has been deceased and that could be rather embarrassing.

Since your card is more or less temporary, my suggestion is to use it often and wisely to help you when you need it most.

PLENTY OF FROGS

How long do you grieve before it's appropriate to date again? A year? A few years? I have come to find out there is no specific time frame. Everyone grieves at a different rate. I must say, from what I have observed, and from my own experience, men seem ready to date quicker than women. I feel women are just more independent by nature.

I have always been a fiercely independent woman, however, I became more so after Jim died. (I thank my mother for that trait.) If you weren't strong before your spouse passed away, you will become strong. Here is what I say is the difference between myself and other women: "I don't need a man, I want a man." Huge difference.

I had both men and women in my bereavement group who literally swore that they would never date again. They said they lost the loves of their lives and that they didn't see a point in ever trying to find that kind of love and bond with someone else. Surprise! Not only have they all been on dates and in relationships, several actually fell in love! Justin, especially, fell head over heels in love and he was the most adamant of the group that said he would never, ever find love again.

Unfortunately, there are so many issues that go hand-in-hand with dating, and even more when dating a widow/widower. Does your new significant other have children? If so, how will your kids get along with their kids? Will you become this new, blended family? How soon into a relationship do you introduce the children? If they don't have kids or their kids are grown, will they be understanding of your situation? Will they want to be involved with your children or have they "been there, done that" and frankly don't want to do it again? So many issues.

I have, for whatever reason, mostly dated men with no children. It's not that I was actively seeking them; it just happened. I must say these men were clueless and incredibly selfish so, inevitably, we would break up because they just didn't get it. The men I have dated have been nice to my girls, one even got somewhat close to them. But no man, in their eyes, or mine for that matter, will ever replace their father so they are very guarded.

I was, and still am, very selective of who I introduce to my girls. I'm not as protective now because they are older. I want them to see you can love again and have a life even though your spouse is gone. Even without a new spouse you can be happy again in a whole new life. Maybe not the one you envisioned, but a good life nonetheless.

Looking back now, it's ironic that I used to say to Jim all the time, when we were curled up in bed, "I'm so happy I'll never have to be out there again in the dating scene." Little did I know that I would, indeed, be out there again and a great deal sooner than I thought. Yet, I wasn't prepared for how awful it truly is, especially in this day and age, or at my age.

When you marry, you are often relatively young. As time goes by, you grow old together. That is a natural progression. You come to accept your spouse's heath issues as you progress through life and the aging process. That is normal. When you start dating again in your forties, fifties and sixties, or beyond, you will, more than likely, have some health issues of your own and inevitably you will have to fill your new partner in on your maladies.

When I met Bryon, he learned about all about my health issues, as there were days they could not stay hidden. The first night he stayed over, I saw his pill bottles and inquired what the medications were, which is how I learned about his high blood pressure. At our age, you're bound to have some health issues.

My girlfriend, Colleen, recently asked me about Bryon and when I told her he had high blood pressure, bad knees and a bad hip from years of playing football, she asked why I would want to be with someone like that as I would end up taking care of him down the road. I was shocked and saddened. Everyone, and I mean EVERYONE, has health issues at my age; no one is perfectly untainted by illness or injury.

What are you supposed to do when you start dating at my age? Should you ask your prospective significant other to list their ailments? Fill out a health questionnaire?

I recently heard a comedian do a bit about dating later in life. Here's what he said:

"I met this woman on line. We chatted, clicked and decided to go to dinner. When I picked her up I asked her what food she was in the mood for. When she said Mexican, I replied, can we stop at a drugstore first?"

Obviously, he had to buy antacids to tame his stomach during their date. This is no joke. Trust me: dating at my age is another ballgame.

Being a widow/widower is so much different than being a divorcee. When you are a widow/widower, you are responsible for your children 24/7. I'll say that again, because it bears repeating: 24/7. So, alone time, unless your children are older, is close to impossible. You might get a few precious hours together with someone you care for at their place, but overnights are pretty much out of the question.

Even if your relationship progresses to the point where they are not only sleeping over, but sleeping in your bed, sex with children in rooms next to yours is so much different than "no kids sex".

All the restrictions can and have put a strain on my relationships over the years. I must admit, most of my dates, if not all, weren't happy that I had my daughters every weekend. No spur of the moment trips; no wine tastings during the day. No afternoon quickies. My weekends, especially as my girls got older, revolved around their sports and other activities. Through this experience, I have gained an even greater admiration for single moms and dads.

In addition, some people find it easier dealing with an ex, as opposed to a ghost. When you're a widow/widower, your new significant other might have a jealous ex to deal with; however, they have to deal with the fact that you loved this person and that you would more than likely still be together had he or she not passed away. Is that easier or harder?

Also, your new partner has to deal with your ex in-laws. Frankly, that's a lot to ask of anyone. My former mother-in-law and her family have always been very gracious to the men I have dated over the years, for which I am very fortunate and thankful. All the relationships, with the exception of one, didn't mind that they had to deal with a ghost, because, basically, he wasn't around, which was all they cared about. These men never really took into account that I didn't want to leave that person. He left me.

My beau, Bryon, feels my husband's presence in my life even though I have insisted on numerous occasions that I am living in the present, not the past and I want, and am trying, to move forward.

Your loved one will never truly be gone, just tucked away in the corner of your mind and heart forever.

In addition, I still call my husband my husband when I speak about him because, to me, he was never an ex. Is this fair to my new significant other? Absolutely not. Recently, my friend from my writing group, Mary, suggested that I refer to him as my late husband which is what I've been calling him ever since.

Brilliant.

What do you call the male person you are dating at my age? "My boyfriend" sounds too immature. My man friend? Oh dear God, no! My soul mate is a bit extreme. My life partner is a bit premature. I polled my writers' group and we decided beau or significant other fits best at this stage of life.

About eight months after my late husband died, an ex-boyfriend named Andy reappeared out of the blue. He was actually the first person to ask for my hand in marriage when I was 21 years old. I initially said yes, then ultimately said no. Dating, soon after Jim died was the furthest thing from my mind. However, because we had a history, it was very easy going back to dating with him, as it was comfortable and familiar. However, there were significant reasons why we originally broke up and, while you would think those issues would resolve themselves after twenty years, sadly they did not. So we broke up yet again and I found myself ready to date others.

Here are the good and bad parts about dating someone you dated many years ago. The good part is that they know you, know your faults and have seen you naked. The bad part is that they know you, know your faults and now they are going to see you naked after twenty-five years and two babies!

The first time we slept together, this time around, I insisted it be dark as I didn't want him to see my body as it looks now. Though I don't have a bad body, especially for someone my age, it's definitely different than my 20-year-old body! You just have to get over it; they want you, no matter what you think or they wouldn't be there.

Before you start dating, remember this: Everyone has baggage, especially after forty. Some people have carry-on, others suitcases, and a few have steamer trunks. Pick the one you feel you can help unpack!

So, how do you meet men at my age? Well, there aren't too many choices. It's not like you're going to go bar hopping, certainly not at this stage of your life. Meeting someone in the grocery or book stores only happens in the movies. Forget friends. They don't want to introduce you to anyone because they don't want to be responsible if it doesn't work out, so don't even ask.

So, what's left? Two very scary words: Internet dating.

First, let me say that it's truly mind boggling as to how many Internet dating sites there are. You have the big ones which are always advertised and charge you forty-five dollars a month or more, to smaller ones and, finally, to the obscure. At each site you will find plenty of frogs.

I started with one site, then eventually worked my way through a few; and amazingly, you see the same people on multiple sites or on the same site for years! This is not encouraging.

Unfortunately, in the end, all sites are all the same, so if you are going to go on one, choose one that costs little or no money. Also know up front that the process is very time consuming, so if you're not serious or you don't have a lot of free time, you might want to rethink your decision.

But where do you begin? First, you create a profile. This is a truly daunting task. You start by answering questions. Are you single, divorced, separated or widowed? What's your income? Education? Do you have children? Do you smoke? And my personal favorite, what's your body type: slender, average, athletic, a few extra pounds or, recently added, big and beautiful? Yikes. Once you've answered all their questions, you have to write an essay telling your potential dates what you're looking for, what your interests are and what you would like to do on a first date. If you think the questions are hard, think again.

Next comes the even harder part: uploading a picture. What picture? I don't know about you, but I'm not particularly photogenic. How should I be dressed? Fancy? Casually? You want to look attractive, but not too attractive. There are actually photos of men without their shirts on. Oh dear Lord. So, you have a choice, you can either go through your current pictures on your phone or your camera, if you have any, or, God forbid even worse, you can take a selfie. You pick one, post it, and hope for the best.

Next come responses. It's like being a gardener; you have to weed through your options. I guess I should be thankful that I received responses, plural. You read them, you look at their photos, read their profiles and you decide to answer one, even two. They email back. You email or instant message back and forth for a day or so.

 Now, they want to call you. You exchange numbers. You talk to them. They sound nice. But are they really nice or are they just saying all the things they think you want to hear?

Some people like to write or talk for weeks before actually meeting. Why? I think they are trying to seduce your mind first. The mind as we all know, is a very powerful organ.

Finally, after all the back and forth, you decide to meet a prospect but where? I've met dates at bars, restaurants, diners, coffee shops, malls and even the park.

Next you find yourself sitting in a diner wondering which one he is. You've seen their picture but do they actually look like their picture? I can tell you from personal experience that is extremely rare. Perhaps they've seen you and decided you weren't what they expected and took off. Usually, within ten minutes you find yourself face to face with an older, shorter, heavier version of the person you saw and read about. Did he think I wouldn't notice that we are standing eye to eye and I'm not even in heels? Five foot, ten inches, I think not! Did they think you wouldn't notice that they looked ten years older than their picture and are perhaps twenty pounds heavier? What the hell were they thinking? Perhaps they thought all the witty banter you shared prior to meeting would cover up the fact that they have already lied to you. Not a great way to start a relationship.

Don't be surprised, but I feel particularly bad for men because a lot of women will go out with numerous guys just to get a free meal or drinks. My cousin, Pete, told me a story about a woman he took out to dinner. She ordered clams four ways and a glass of expensive vodka. He got a kiss on the cheek and never heard from her again. I always split my checks because I felt we both worked hard for our money and besides, that's just not my style.

So, are there plenty of frogs? Yes, and in some cases, there are plenty of freaks.

BEFORE AND AFTER

When I say before and after, I mean who I was prior to Jim's death and who I have become since his death. Here are some of the ways I have changed and grown and, I must say, most, if not all, are for the better.

However, with that being said, understand that I am a changed person ten years later; I am not the person I was prior to his death or even a few years after. I have morphed into a different person. His death changed me and I had no choice. If I had written this book right after Jim's death, it would probably be more horrific and much more sorrowful. I have moved through the five stages of grief many, many times. The person writing this book is the person I have become.

While I was always a strong, independent woman, I became much more so after my late husband's death. Actually, maybe too independent. Ten years later I have a hard time accepting help, especially from a man. I have been doing everything myself for so long that a lot of what I do now is second nature. In the beginning, when I would do one of Jim's chores, I would think he should be doing it and I would be extremely mad and resentful. Now, when I do something he used to do, I don't even think about it anymore; it's just one of my chores - something I do automatically without even a second thought.

When Bryon wants to plow my driveway or take my car for an oil change, I actually fight with him, saying I can do it myself, I've been doing it for years, no big deal; however, to him, it IS a big deal. He wants to help lighten my load, to be the man and while I eventually let him, it's a struggle to give up my autonomy. While these aren't bad things and are actually quite wonderful, it's going to take time getting used to letting go.

Before, I was always terrified of death even though I have a strong faith and believe in Heaven. Now, I am no longer afraid to die. While I will miss my girls, Bryon, family and friends and all the earthly pleasures in life, I truly believe that I will be able to see my loved ones on earth while being with my deceased loved ones in Heaven. That is a truly amazing and comforting thought as I originally had been consumed and saddened with the idea of my death since I was a child.

I now know that as much as I adore my house, my neighbors and my community, in order for me to move on, not only in my life but my relationship with Bryon, I will inevitably sell my home. I don't have to; I want to. This will be extremely difficult for me, as I always envisioned being a grandmother here and having my daughters bring their children to their childhood home. But my house will no longer be a home to me once my girls are out on their own.

My house is extremely comfortable and I love it. It's filled with so many wonderful memories. Jim redid the house room by room when we moved in, to make it our home, no longer someone else's. My girls' births, taking their first steps, the countless parties, birthdays and holidays; the house is part of the various stages of my girls' lives.

However, this is also the house where Jim took his life, so there are sad and horrific memories here too. Believe it or not, after ten years that dreadful incident does not outweigh the good times that his house has provided for 21 years, so it will be difficult to leave it someday.

It's the new me, as I don't like change, never did. I only moved four times in my life and I was the only one in my family who didn't want my mom to sell our childhood home after my dad died. I was devastated, even though I was long on my own and living in New York City. Before this happened, I imagined living in our home well into my old age, but not anymore. I know now that I don't need to live in our home to hold on to the memories; they will live on forever in my heart.

I used to be a perfectionist to the point of driving myself and Jim crazy. When we would have guests over, I would cook and clean for days making everything picture perfect. I would wash my floors before everyone got there just to have them trampled upon moments later. Even what should have been a simple barbecue with family or friends would turn into a major feast; your average barbecue would simply not do. Jim would always say, "Why don't we just get a keg and a wedge?"

Oh the horror!

I remember having Samantha's family party for her fifth birthday four months after Jim died and I actually apologized for just having hamburgers and hot dogs and some salads. Of course, I made every topping imaginable for those hamburgers, hot dogs and salads but, to me, it still wasn't enough.

Now, ten years later, while I still turn it out "big time" when guests are coming, I no longer go into full-blown "Marguerite mode" (my mother), as Jim affectionately used to call my pre-company craziness. I no longer wash the floors, re-vacuum, clean upstairs, pull weeds, or stress about the weather. I am more relaxed because I no longer sweat the small stuff. There's no fun in being perfect. While I don't necessarily like the cleaning and prepping, I do enjoy the cooking and the day so much more now because I actually sit and enjoy the people I love.

Perfection is one of my biggest character defects and one I've had a long time, but I am evolving and I pass this newly developed wisdom on to my daughters. I clean less and enjoy more now. I know that may sound funny to you but for those that know me, that's a huge change. I can now sit in a chair in my living room and read even though I see a layer of dust on my mantelpiece. The old Kim would have jumped up and dusted it immediately. Not anymore. I'd much rather enjoy my book.

My girls and I used to feel obligated to go to the cemetery for Jim's birthday, anniversary and all holidays. Not anymore. We go now when we want, not when we have to or when people think we should. We don't do it out of obligation anymore; we do it out of love. Huge difference.

I am sure his mom and family aren't happy about that but they are welcome to go anytime they wish. Besides, I know his soul is long gone and we no longer have to sit at a cemetery to honor or remember him; we can do that anywhere.

I used to always live in the past or the future; if I wasn't thinking about one, I was dwelling about the other. Now, I live totally in the moment. I go to bed thanking God for the day and wake up thankful that I'm alive to live another. I make a conscious effort to have a good day and try and stay positive. I do a lot of random acts of kindness, thanks to my friend Suzanne, which makes me smile. You never know when it's going to be your last day, so I make the best out of the one I'm in. I say I'm sorry often, and when I'm wrong about something, I actually admit it. I rarely hold a grudge; not an easy feat for a Scorpio Italian woman. Again, life's too short.

Mostly, I give love, hugs and say I love you more freely now. I grew up in a house where PDA was a no-no. I tell my daughters twice a day, once before they leave for school and before they go to sleep that I love them. I don't ever want to regret not saying those words, ever.

So, looking back, the after me is actually an improved version of the before me. I was able to move through the worst thing imaginable and come out okay on the other side. I found strength when I thought I just couldn't go on. I amazed not only my friends but myself. I guess sometimes it takes the death of someone close to you to realize the important things in life. That you can persevere.

Lesson learned.

--The End--

ACKNOWLEDGMENTS

I want to thank Linda Spear who selflessly gave of her time to teach my writing class week after week for over three years. There wouldn't be a book without her prodding me along and never giving up on me. I will forever be grateful to her for her never-ending support and patience with me, a first-time author.

Many thanks to my Friday morning writing group, for all their wonderful suggestions, kind words and most of all friendship. I am truly honored to know these extraordinary women/writers, Mary Davidson, Donna Manfredi Murphy, Stacie Vourakis, Faye DeSanto, Karen Phelps, Tanya Pennella, and a special thanks to Christine Adler.

A huge thank you to my family, my sister, my best friend, Laura Castellano, who rocked my cradle when she was hiding out from our mom, and rocked me to sleep the night Jim died. You have always been there for me and I can't thank you enough. Also, thank you for shooting the photos on my book jacket! My oldest sibling, Karen Castellano who, having worked for Andy Warhol at Interview Magazine, helped with a couple of chapters of initial editing. Also, I must thank my brother, Peter Castellano, who produced facts when my memory wouldn't let me go there.

To my bereavement buddies: Candace, Leigh, Justin, Keith, Linda, Shari, and Shannon and my non-bereavement group friends who also lost their spouses to suicide, Tricia and Jim. Your stories helped shape my story.

Thank you to all the friends I mentioned in my book; you know who you are. Of course, I must thank my dearest friends in the world who have always been there for me. To my two friends whom I have known since I was five, Bobbi (Barbara) Rogoff and Colleen Deery. Bobbi, for your ability to make me laugh like no one else, for your drive-by doughnuts and your belief in me that I could not only write this book but that it would help others. Colleen for trying to make me a good girl and always telling me the truth. My third oldest friend, Carolyn Newman, for being her own warrior and now mine. My NYC friend, Amy Germain, who taught me how to live life to the fullest and to not sweat the small stuff and who helped me with my second edition. To Valerie Dellamedaglia who helped me get through some of the roughest parts. Michelle Schmitt for always keeping it real. And a special thanks to Juliette Fourgeot Sussmann, my dearest friend, neighbor, birthday buddy, Scorpio twin. I wouldn't be where I am today without you and your beautiful family helping us through such a life-changing event. Each of you incredible women played a huge role when Jim died and continue to do so now, ten years later. I love you all.

And especially to my deceased parents; my beloved beautiful mom, Marguerite, who made me the strong, independent woman I am today. My beloved dad, Peter, who I got my generous spirit from; he was and will forever be my hero.

And finally to my beau, Bryon Burger for his patience, unwavering support and mostly, love. You are my calm, my man and I am so grateful we found each other.

69289258R00086

Made in the USA
Columbia, SC
17 April 2017